Happy Birth, Happy Baby

Happy Birth, Happy Baby

Kelly Palmer

BOOKS

Winchester, UK
Washington, USA

First published by O-Books, 2018
O-Books is an imprint of John Hunt Publishing Ltd., No. 3 East St., Alresford,
Hampshire SO24 9EE, UK
office1@jhpbooks.net
www.johnhuntpublishing.com

For distributor details and how to order please visit the 'Ordering' section on our website.

Text copyright: Kelly Palmer 2017

ISBN: 978 1 78535 717 6
978 1 78535 718 3 (ebook)
Library of Congress Control Number: 2017942027

A CIP catalogue record for this book is available from the British Library.

Design: Stuart Davies

Printed and bound by CPI Group (UK) Ltd, Croydon, CR0 4YY, UK

We operate a distinctive and ethical publishing philosophy in
all areas of our business, from our global network of authors to
production and worldwide distribution.

Contents

For Mimi Cooper, midwife extraordinaire.

Introduction

*As long as she lives, a woman will never forget how she was
made to feel at her births.*
Anna Verwaal

Birth matters.

For the baby, the mother, and the world. A calm birth in a
comforting environment has myriad positive and far-reaching
effects for both mother and baby, including a vastly decreased
chance of post-natal depression. Positive birth practices lead to
less pain, often shorter labours and an empowering rather than
traumatic experience. Women's bodies instinctively know how
to birth, and when left alone to do so childbirth can be a deeply
spiritual and transformative experience. Midwives, doulas,
mothers and grandmothers the world over know this, have
known it for centuries.

So how have we got here?

Birth is regularly spoken about as an agonising and scary
process and we women swap negative birth experiences with
gusto. Programs such as *One Born Every Minute* which primarily
show highly medicalised births as the norm (which sadly, they
now often are) have a lot to answer for.

As of 2016, only sixty per cent of Western women have natural
vaginal deliveries, the majority of which take place in hospital
and are heavily monitored. Caesareans, gruelling inductions
and instrumental delivery which almost always entails an
episiotomy – being 'cut' – are increasing year upon year. The
results of this, as we shall see, are devastating on a personal and
global level. And the rates of PTSD after birth, directly related to
medical intervention, are increasing rapidly.

Yet there's hope on the horizon. Thanks to groups of dedicated
women – and some remarkably intuitive men – birth is being

1

reclaimed. Awareness is growing. Individual women are coming back to their instincts, back to their bodies, and asking for, if not demanding, the births they intuitively know to be right for them and their baby. Medical establishments are slowly, but surely, catching up, as practices such as immediate skin-to-skin contact and delayed cord clamping become routine. (As if we needed to be told the most natural thing in the world – to hold our babies after birthing them!) Midwives are speaking up and fighting back against cuts and uncompassionate practices. Women are employing doulas to advocate for them and provide the comfort and companionship during birth that would once have been commonplace. More and more mothers-to-be are turning to hypnobirthing rather than or as well as clinical pain relief choices, and finding that labour doesn't have to be agonising after all. Researchers every day are discovering that we had it right all along.

The natural birth movement has been around for a while, largely on the fringes, but gaining more and more ground in recent years. It gained real momentum, particularly in the US (which still has the highest maternal mortality rates in the developed world, which have only increased as birth has become more and more medicalised) in the 60s and 70s, a time when consciousness raising in general and feminism in particular were at the forefront of the collective psyche. The movement emerged in response to the increasing medicalisation of birth, spearheaded not only by mothers themselves but also the doctors and nurses involved in their care, who witnessed the results of over-intervention.

Until the nineteenth century women generally laboured at home, under the care of midwives. Modernity saw a shift to doctor-led, hospital-based care, and anaesthetics began to be used initially for the nobility only but later becoming widespread. Women were told to lay on their backs to birth, a position that made delivery difficult for mother and baby, but gave better access to the usually male doctor. Awareness of the dangers of anaesthetics began to grow and in the 1930s Grantly Dick-Read, an obstetrician, published *Childbirth Without Fear* and became an advocate for the return of natural childbirth. In the 50s and 60s French obstetrician Michel Odent began to campaign for natural birth, water births and the importance of maternal health and well-being, including relaxation during the birth itself. The La Leche League was formed to promote breastfeeding and Sister Mary Stella introduced the concept of family-centred maternity care. The women's movement began to question the way women's bodies were objectified, not just in the media but in medicine too. The natural childbirth movement came into its own as women started reclaiming both their bodies and their birthing practices. The 70s saw Ina May Gaskin, an independent midwife in the US, begin attending births at The Farm, a midwifery centre she founded that was and remains famous for its holistic approach to birth. To this day The Farm has super-low rates of interventions and mortality.

There was a darker side to the movement, however, as some campaigners began to use language that suggested women were somehow failing or not living up to their role if they didn't have a drug-free home birth and breastfeed for the first two years. Childbirth became politicised, with mothers caught between the coldly clinical and over-intervention of obstetricians and doctors in often short-staffed and underfunded hospitals on the one hand, and radical 'natural at all costs' advocates on the other. Many women were left feeling bewildered, confused and like they just couldn't get it right.

Thankfully in recent years the 'positive birth movement' has found more of a balance, placing mothers back where they have every right to be: at the centre of their own birth, making informed choices and being treated with respect. This can also be termed woman-centred birth, a term that resonates strongly for me. The woman is placed back where she has always been: at the centre of birth. As the active agent in the process, not a passive player. Midwives, obstetricians, birth partners, surgeons… they don't deliver and birth babies. Mothers do.

Birth matters. Imagine a whole generation of babies born to happy, calm mothers, their first experiences outside the womb being warm and nurturing, not frightening or clinical. Happy births mean happy babies. Happy babies have a greater likelihood of growing up to be happy and resilient adults.

Changing birth can change the world.

My Story

My first son was born in 2001. I was nineteen, knew nothing about babies, and did whatever my doctor told me. I was advised to have an epidural when I asked if it would hurt. My mother regaled me with tales of how horrendous my own birth had been. I went into labour at home, and spent five hours sitting in the bathroom, instinctively breathing through contractions while talking on the phone to my friend. My son's father was putting up our new wardrobes, and I was determined he would finish them before we went to hospital, in spite of his protestations. I remember being surprised that the contractions, even though they were coming every three minutes, weren't really painful at all, just intense tightening feelings. We finally called a cab to the hospital when my waters broke (funnily enough, just as my young husband had finished the wardrobes and sat down for a well-earned cup of tea!). I was excited, even euphoric, and preoccupied with checking that everything we needed was in my hospital bag.

As soon as we got to the hospital, it all changed. I was examined by a very brusque midwife with rough fingers while a student midwife looked on. I was between six and seven centimetres dilated. So far, I thought, this had been pretty easy. Then I was told, 'It's going to get a lot worse; if you want an epidural, have one now.' I agreed. Never being a fan of needles, I found the epidural procedure the most painful thing that had happened during my birth up to that point, and began to feel scared, exposed and wishing I had just stayed at home. My labour then proceeded to slow right down and it was eleven hours before my son was born, during which I felt intimidated by the less than compassionate midwife, and was shouted at by my mother when I became very vocal at the pushing stage. I felt bewildered and frightened throughout, only experiencing something of the innate power of birth when my son began to crown and I pushed him out into the world, suddenly elated.

He was whisked away from me while I was stitched up (I tore, having flat out refused an episiotomy, the only moment where my natural assertiveness kicked in) and I lay there feeling very exposed and desperately longing to hold my son. Eventually, when we had been moved on to the postnatal ward and everyone had gone home, I sat cuddling this wondrous little being, overwhelmed with a rush of love like nothing I had ever felt. I remember feeling intensely protective, as though I needed to keep him safe from the medical staff that had pushed and prodded us and separated us at the time when every natural instinct screamed that we should be together. I developed postnatal depression twelve weeks later and often thought back to that initial separation, feeling tearful for reasons I couldn't explain.

Four years later, after a succession of miscarriages, I was pregnant with my daughter. I was determined there would be no epidural this time, no being strapped flat to a bed. I remembered the first hours of my son's birth, when I had instinctively moved into comfortable positions and phoned a trusted friend for support. I knew there was a better way than my first experience. I wrote a birth plan, and opted for a water birth.

It didn't happen. After a stressful pregnancy (I was in an emotionally toxic relationship by this point) my waters broke far too early, and I had to be induced for mine and the baby's safety. At this point, I think it's important to stress that, in spite of the problems unnecessary medical interventions cause, when used appropriately in an emergency situation, the positive side of medical science comes to the fore. This book will also explore ways in which even the most medicalised of births can be transformed into a calmer and life-affirming experience.

Back to my induction. Expecting that it could be hours or even days before I went into labour, everyone was sent home after I was given the necessary gel and I was given a comfortable bed, a cup of tea and told to get some sleep; I would be examined again in the morning. I went to sleep, and woke up in the early hours in the middle of a contraction. When I called the midwife she said I would probably only be a few centimetres dilated. Upon discovering I was nearly seven, I was rushed up to the labour ward. My daughter was born just a few hours later, after a short, intense but joyful labour during which I chatted away happily with the easy-going, hands-off midwife. I needed no stitches and was walking around half an hour after giving birth. I felt powerful, I felt strong, and couldn't understand why I had never been told that having a baby could be like this.

I again later developed postnatal depression, but this time I didn't count the birth as a factor, rather the stress of trying to manage university with a toddler, a newborn and an unsupportive partner.

Ten years later I had remarried and trained as a psychotherapist following my own recovery from trauma. A result of that trauma was pregnancy loss. I grieved hard, and as much as I (on the surface at least) recovered and fell deeply in love with my second husband, I was adamant I would not get pregnant again. Then I unexpectedly, in spite of the birth control, conceived my youngest son. Somehow I knew the moment it happened, although no one believed me until it was confirmed a month later. I also, underneath the inevitable anxiety, had the inevitable feeling that my baby would be okay. I knew exactly what I wanted for this baby's birth: a water birth with natural pain relief, as little intervention as possible and my husband by my side. I used my prior training in hypnotherapy and a daily mindfulness practice to navigate the ups and downs of pregnancy and bought a copy of the bestselling *Mindful Hypnobirthing* by birth practitioner Sophie Fletcher. I wrote a comprehensive birth plan, and when I was told I was considered a high-risk pregnancy, used my increased knowledge to effectively make my case to be reclassified as low risk and admitted to the local midwife-led birthing centre complete with birthing pool.

Once again, it didn't happen. When my baby hadn't been delivered at 41 weeks and showed no sign of budging, I was informed I would need an induction. Only later in the course of my research as a birth practitioner did I discover that things may have been better left alone. Remembering how easy my daughter's induction had been, I expected things to be similar.

Cue three days of off-the-chart contractions and no dilation, on a grubby ward with rude staff who could only offer me paracetamol! Thank the heavens for the hypnobirthing and mindfulness techniques I had learned. I spent most of the three days in a warm bath, my husband next to me (he was amazingly supportive, proving that men can and do have a role at birth) breathing, meditating and visualising. Amazingly, when I was 'in the zone' there was no pain, only an otherworldly sense of peace. Only when I was interrupted by medical staff for yet another monitoring session or brusque vaginal examination did I experience pain.

On the third day, however, still not at all dilated, my body was exhausted, and I gave in and agreed to a syntocinon drip (an artificial form of oxytocin). I was pushing within a few hours, but things weren't happening quick enough for the obstetrician's liking and she came in to the rather lovely labour room (it was painted a soft yellow with purple butterflies on the wall; I had been using them as a self-hypnosis focal point) and started talking about forceps and episiotomies. I had written this on my birth plan as a definite no-no, preferring a C-section in the event of an emergency. She didn't even address me, instead she talked over my head and referred to me as 'she'. In that moment, after having stayed mostly calm and even excited throughout what was certainly a feat of endurance, testament to the innate power of the female body-mind, I felt my spirit sink. How, I thought, could another woman be so callous?

Thankfully, a midwife I can only describe as a gift from Mama

Nature came in, all round cheeks and booming laugh, and all but demanded the obstetrician leave the room. She then turned to me, winked and said, 'Let's do this.' Her name was Mimi Cooper, and I will never forget her. I found a strength I didn't realise I possessed and ten minutes later my son was lying on my breast, gazing up at me and making his first whimpers, while my husband cuddled us both. I don't have the words to express the absolute power and joy of that moment. I felt absolutely triumphant, and madly in love.

I didn't get postnatal depression.

This final birth taught me a lot, including:

- The God/Mama Nature-given innate, intense, spiritual and transformative power of the birth process.
- That a woman's body is designed to birth. There may be incidences where help is needed, but ultimately the woman is the central actor.
- That with a calming environment, a supportive birth partner and self-empowering techniques, birth sensations may be intense, but are a lot more manageable.
- The amazing difference a woman-centred, compassionate midwife or other medical professional can make.
- The importance of supportive, loving and non-judgmental birth partners.
- That the current medical model of birth is fear-led and completely counter-intuitive to the natural birth process, often using interventions designed for emergencies as routine.
- That I wanted to do everything I could to empower women to reclaim their own birthing experiences. More than wanted; I felt *called*.

About This Book

I've divided this book into three sections to explore the different impact a mindful, woman-centred and positive birth can have: on the mother, the baby and society as a whole. I start with the mother because all else follows on from there; happy mothers mean happy babies.

The first section will look at the impact of birth as a transformative, psychological and spiritual process and how you can begin to change the story you have about birth and visualise the birth you want. Then we will look at a variety of techniques, resources and ways of communicating with midwives and doctors to ensure they are on board with your birth plan. We will also look at the role your oxytocin levels play in birth and how this is key to having a more calm and relaxed labour. We will then look at challenges some women face from unwanted intervention and previous trauma, and how you can heal and empower yourself to overcome these.

The second section will look at the physiological impact and the psychological effects of birth on your baby. We will discuss how the birth process may affect future health and the importance of passing on your microbes to your newborn. I will also give brief discussions of skin-to-skin contact, delayed cord clamping, Vitamin K and the recent trend for lotus births. Bonding between mother and baby and what happens on a psychological level will be explored as will the phenomenon of birth memories. I will also share a practice for bonding with baby in late pregnancy. This section will finish with a look at the immediate postnatal period and the importance of the 'babymoon' as well as the mother's needs for physical and psychological healing.

In the final section we will look at the widespread impact of birth: culturally and evolutionary, including fascinating new research. In the last chapter I will introduce you to some of the leading figures in the birth world should you wish to explore further or even get involved.

Although in each section I provide lots of information, primarily this book is a practical one; designed to help women bring this transformative power into their own births, or reframe the ones they have already had. I will share the practices and techniques that helped me and that I use with other women in my work as a hypnobirthing and mindfulness practitioner and doula. Even if you don't have time to read the book cover to cover, I strongly recommend you try the exercises. I will also share stories and anecdotes from mythology, history and most importantly other women of today, as well as provide resources to guide further exploration. You will find specific resources at the end of each chapter that will lead you to books, websites and documentaries that will inspire your own birth journey.

In conjunction to this book you get free access at www. happybirthhappybaby.co.uk which includes downloadable meditations, self-hypnosis tracks, downloadable e-books and workbooks. You can also hit me up on Twitter @ happybirthhappybaby.

It is my deepest wish that this work helps inspire your own birth journey, improve your confidence, help you heal and move on from any past birth trauma and have a happy birth and a happy baby!

Part One – Happy Birth, Happy Mama

When the baby is born, the mother is also born.
Rajneesh

Chapter One – Birth is Powerful

Birth is the epicentre of a woman's power.
Ani DiFranco

Childbirth is one of the most empowering initiations a person can go through, and one that is unique to the female sex. In Jungian archetypal psychology, birth is the ultimate psychological and spiritual experience.

Of course, that doesn't mean it's easy. Birth is a soul searching, body shaking feat of endurance that requires a woman to dig to the very depths of her inner resources and come out the other side forever changed. All the more reason why this deserves respect, compassion and recognition. Sadly in today's Western, medicalised culture, birth is seen as something to 'get through' and 'get over' with hopefully as little mess as possible. And women who have had profound, even euphoric birth experiences often find their voices go unheard amid the over-representation of medicalised birth and women swapping ever more horrific birth stories with one another.

'It was agony,' 'I thought I was dying,' 'I'm never going through that again,' we tell each other with solemn shakes of the head, sighing and nudging each other when a friend gets pregnant for the first time and announces she wants a natural, drug-free birth. 'You'll change your mind,' we tell her. I've been guilty of this myself. And we do this not just to each other, but in front of men too, tutting at their unbelievably low pain thresholds and laughing when they say it can't be any worse than a kick to the testicles. (Just to clear this up, they are completely different physiological processes and not comparable.)

Why do we do this? I believe it comes from the deep-down need for recognition, to be heard in a culture that often silences us. We know, on the deepest level of knowing, that birth is vitally important, not just as a biological process but as a psycho-spiritual one, that the way we birth influences us for generations. But in a society that limits our expression of this, we try to communicate its importance in the only way we can, by describing it as excruciating and frightening. We try to convince the males in our lives of our superior pain thresholds as a way to convey the specialness of this event that only the female can participate in, as a way to reclaim the respect our innate powers of creation and birth so richly deserve.

And of course, largely thanks to modern birth practices, sadly our experiences may really be this painful. We will look at the physical sensation of birth more in Chapter Two, but for now let me assure you of this: birth doesn't have to be this way.

It certainly was never designed to be this way. For the most part, the female form is uniquely designed to give birth. I am in no way dismissing the experiences of women who cannot birth, or stating that natural childbirth is never traumatic; nevertheless the fact remains that a healthy woman having a healthy pregnancy has all the resources she needs within her to birth her baby, along with the support of a good midwife and caring birth companion. How amazing would it be if a natural, woman-led birth was the norm, rather than an over-medicalised, sterilised and often traumatic birth experience that leaves many women feeling disempowered? How much more confident would we feel as women if our birthing power and our right to choose was routinely respected?

The right to choose is crucial for a woman to feel she has had a positive birth. For various reasons, some women will decide on an epidural, induction or C-section, and various forms of pain relief. There is nothing wrong with this. It is unwanted and unnecessary intervention, which the mother is often at best coerced into, that creates the problem. I believe passionately in a woman's innate right to make her own childbirth choices, and the natural childbirth movement can in some cases sadly be just as responsible for making women feel they 'aren't doing it right'. My vision for birth is that all women feel confident in their own bodies, that childbirth be respected and recognised for the powerful rite of passage it is, and that women be given accurate and balanced information to make their own choices. Each pregnancy, each mother, each child, is an individual.

Recent studies have illustrated that the following factors are crucial for a woman to experience her birth as positive:

- continuous emotional support
- the sense that she is in control of her own body and choices
- the knowledge to make informed choices about her care, pain relief and any interventions
- a calming, safe environment
- self-empowering techniques to manage the sensations and rhythms of birth
- uninterrupted time with her baby immediately after the birth

Birth as Initiation

We will look at some of these factors in more detail in the next and later chapters, but for now I want to look in more depth about the statement I made at the beginning of this chapter. That childbirth is an empowering initiation. A rite of passage. Rites of passage can be described as being made up of three stages: separation, transition, and return. These stages are present at birth in the following ways:

- Separation – labour begins and the mother enters an altered state, known as 'the birthing zone', essentially retreating from the outside world and drawing her attention inwards to focus on her body and baby. Many labouring women report a feeling of being 'outside time' or of having little sense of time passing. This is a natural process that allows oxytocin – the 'birthing hormone' – to rise and helps labour progress. Anxieties and interventions at this period cause stress hormones to rise instead, interrupting the flow of oxytocin and even impending labour. This makes personal sense to me in light of how my first labour seemed to stall as soon as I went to hospital.

- Transition and transformation – the time during any initiation when we are between phases, and often a time of testing, or the 'darkness before the dawn' in hero/ine stories. In childbirth, psychological transition usually corresponds with the physical transition between the first and second stages of labour. This is a time when the stress hormone cortisol naturally peaks, and the birthing woman may find herself suddenly overwhelmed by sensation and feeling she can't go on. I believe if women were routinely told to expect this stage and given strategies to deal with it childbirth would be a lot less frightening. Then the pushing begins and the baby is born – the time of transformation, the peak experience.

- Return – the baby is (hopefully) on the mother's chest, the placenta being delivered, and the mother gradually returns to her former state of non-pregnant; yet is forever changed.

Understanding fully the powerful nature of birth empowers women and helps relieve the anxiety and feelings of helplessness so many of us feel at a time when we are already vulnerable. That is one of the great paradoxes of the birthing woman: that she is simultaneously at her most powerful and her most vulnerable.

Labour is what is known as a *liminal* time. The word liminal has its roots in an old word for 'threshold' and refers to a 'time between' or a transition phase, often involving a waiting period and a time of transformation. Birth is all of these. Pregnancy and the postnatal period too can be regarded as a time of liminality. During this whole period the woman is 'between times' where her old life has gone and her new one, with the new child, has not yet fully begun. Liminal times are periods of great awakening and creativity, yet also of vulnerability. The failure to mark these times with ritual and respect can lead to feelings of depression and lack of purpose. Add this to lack of sleep, social pressures, possible birth trauma and lack of support and it's not hard to see why rates of post-natal depression are so high in the Western world.

Recently there has been growing interest in rituals around birth and becoming a mother – known often as 'birth rites'. Birth rites may include:

- A 'mother blessing' is the originator of the modern baby shower, with a focus less on gifts and more on showering the mother with blessings and sharing stories and tips to positively prepare her for birth and motherhood. Mother Blessings are becoming popular and there is a guided ritual in the Appendices to help you prepare your own.
- Personal rituals that help the mother in birth, such as affirmations, breathing practices, even dancing and lighting candles or burning certain oils. These are, consciously or otherwise, designed to help the mother find her way into the birthing zone.
- Placenta rituals. Ancient customs such as burying the placenta and planting a small tree above it are being revived, and placenta encapsulation, where the placenta is turned into capsules that are then imbibed by the mother, is becoming increasingly popular. Ingesting the placenta has long been an accepted part of traditional Chinese medicine, and it is believed that the nutrients in the placenta help the woman return to full health after birth, increase milk production and shrink the uterus

back to normal size. Recent scientific studies have been inconclusive, but rich anecdotal research suggests many women feel benefits from this. As an aside, I've always felt rather squeamish about the placenta, but gained a new respect for it when the midwife at my last birth opened it up to show me the intricate pattern of veins in the middle, which looked exactly like a tree and which she called 'The Tree of Life'.

- Baby namings and blessings. Alternatives to the typical Christening or baptism abound in recent years, often with less of a focus on religious rites and more on wishing both mother and baby health and happiness.
- 'Babymooning'. The first few months after childbirth are also a time of liminality, and in many cultures women are given time to bond with the baby while others – often female relatives – take care of chores and older children. There has been increased recognition of this important phase recently in natural and attachment parenting circles.

Making the effort to build personal rituals into the pregnancy, birth and 'babymoon' can foster a sense of self-care and increased well-being in the mother, and so in the baby. Anthropologists and social scientists have long been aware of the importance of personal and collective ritual for psychological health, particularly during times of transition.

Rituals are, in part, about 'story-making'. Humans are meaning-motivated creatures, and we like events to run along certain narratives, hence why films and novels have certain expectations built into them. The guy gets the girl after some funny mishaps in a romantic comedy, someone always dies in a tear-jerking family drama, a pretty girl gets killed in the opening scenes in a slasher flick... Although real life is seldom as clear cut, we tend to view events in ours and others' lives in the same way. Big life events such as birth, marriage and death come with their own narratives.

Sadly, the modern 'birth story' is often a negative one, with the woman seen as a passive character in the drama. Birth happens to her, rather than being an act she consciously participates in, and the catcher of the baby is cast in the hero role. With this narrative, we could be forgiven for thinking a baby can't possibly be born without a full team of medical staff on hand and an epidural at the ready.

These narratives have a powerful effect on our beliefs and expectations. So one way to alter our beliefs and expectations is to change the narrative, or story, that we're telling ourselves. Recognising birth as a rite of passage and including some of the rituals described above in your experience can help do this. As can taking in positive birth stories. Yes, they exist. Lots of them! You can find some at the back of this book, as well as links in the resource section to sites and publications dedicated to sharing birth stories that educate and empower. Some other ideas are:

- Politely ask female relatives and friends to stop regaling you with tales of how horrific their births were.
- Do some research into positive birth practices in other cultures and countries – the Netherlands in particular.
- Write your own ideal birth story, and read it regularly during your pregnancy, really visualising or imagining the scene in your mind.
- Try the exercises at the end of this section.
- Read creation myths that celebrate the power of birth, such as the one below.

Sumerian Birth Myth

Sumer was one of the world's first advanced civilisations, the forerunner of the Babylonian civilisation of Biblical times. Their creation myth tells that the Goddess Nammu, the Great Mother, created the heavens and earth, birthing them from her own body along with the other gods. Humans were fashioned from the clay of the earth by the trickster god Enki while the birthing goddesses, or Ninmah, oversaw and blessed the process. Humans were made in the image of the gods, including the Goddess's ability to birth from her own body.

Shows childbirth in a whole different light, don't you think? Imagine if we had grown up with that narrative rather than one that told us women were solely responsible for the fall of humankind and as a consequence had been cursed with labour pains? Stories are powerful.

Birth is powerful.

Exercise – Mindfulness Meditation

Try this before the journaling exercise below. Sit comfortably, close your eyes and begin to breathe deeply. Make your exhale a little longer than your inhale. Bring your attention to the breath; the feeling of air coming in and out of your nostrils; the sound it makes. Continue breathing this way for a few minutes. If your attention wanders, it's okay, just bring it back to the breath.

Bring your attention to your body; notice any areas of tension or stress and just breathe into them, feeling any tension dissolve. Now say the word 'birth' to yourself. What happens to your body? Your breath? What images do you see or memories do you recall? Just be aware. Then breathe out, imagining you are letting all this go, and bring your attention back to the breath. When you are ready, answer the following questions.

Exercise – Journaling Questions – What's My Birth Story?

What did my mother tell me about my birth?

What did I hear about childbirth growing up?

How have I seen birth portrayed in the media?

What do my friends say about their births?

How does talking to my midwife or doctor make me feel?

When I think about the birth of my baby, what images and sensations come to mind?

What do I need to believe to feel positive about giving birth?

What beliefs are not helping me?

What would help me?

Birth Art

The creative power of pregnancy and birth often manifests in women's psyche as a surge in their own creativity, and many women report feeling more creative during pregnancy and even, if they can find the time, during the post-natal period. Personally, I started new writing projects within weeks of my births, overcome by a sudden rush of ideas and an urge to write at every available opportunity.

In recent years the ancient tradition of birth art – art, sculptures or mandalas depicting birthing women and used as visual aids for pregnant and labouring women – has been revived and there are some beautiful examples of this in the resource section. Creating your own birth art is a lovely way to both harness the extra creative energy of pregnancy and also start to change your internal birth story. The exercises below will help you to do both, even if you don't see yourself as an artist. Exercises like this are deceptively simple, yet have a real and profound effect on our well-being.

Exercise – Creating a Birth Vision Board

Get some natural childbirth magazines or resources, a pinboard, canvas or even just a large sheet of paper, and make a collage out of any images and words that speak to you about the power of birth and your ideal birth experience. If you would like some ideas, there are some great examples on Pinterest. Make it as bold and colourful and meaningful to you as you can. Put it somewhere you can see it regularly and add to it as you wish as your pregnancy progresses. You can even use it as a visual aid during the birth itself.

If you are interested in the more spiritual aspects of birth and want to capture this in your birth art, listen to the guided meditation below before you create your art. This is suitable for women going through or approaching any new phase in their life. You can download this from www.happybirthhappybaby.co.uk or alternatively record the script below and play it back to yourself.

Exercise – Journey to Birth Visualisation

Just get yourself comfortable now... and now let your eyes find something on that wall... some spot or corner or a small object... and let your eyes rest on that point while you listen to the sound of my voice... hold your eyes open... and just look at that spot or that point... for a few moments... keep focusing on that spot... and your eyelids become heavy... heavier and heavier... blinking more and more... you can feel those eyelids becoming so heavy... but you just keep them open now... they may begin to water... that's okay... just keep them open... keep focusing... heavier and heavier... even though you want to close them you can keep them open for a few moments longer... and now close your eyes down... and as you close your eyes down you feel a wave of relaxation sweep through your entire body...

Now just focus on your breathing... breathing deeply... as you become so very deeply relaxed... breathing in... and breathing out... feeling your lungs and stomach expand as you breathe in... and your body relax so very deeply as you breathe out... relaxing more and more...

And now become aware of the quality of that relaxation...

and imagine that relaxation spreading through the whole of your body... sweeping down from the top of your head to the tips of your toes... like a wave of relaxation... letting go... let go and relax every muscle in your body... that's right... really feel that relaxation from the crown of your head to the tips of your toes... feel how very good it feels to be this deeply relaxed...

And as deep as you are now... you can go ten times deeper. In a moment I am going to ask you to open your eyes... and then when you close them again you will go ten times deeper... so very deeply relaxed... relaxed in body and mind...

When you are ready I want you to imagine... in as much detail as is right for you now... a stone staircase that takes you down to a special place... a safe place that is just for you... it feels inviting to you and you go down... a step at a time... as I count from ten to one... and as I do so you can imagine yourself going down... a step at a time... going deeper and deeper... ten... nine... eight... see yourself going down... seven... six... hear your footsteps on the stairs, feel the stairs beneath your feet, and imagine yourself going deeper still... five... four... three... two... one... you step down and you can find yourself in a cave... with cool sand underneath your feet... surrounded by ancient rock walls... you feel safe here... and you can explore and take in all of the wonderful things there are to experience... all of the sights and sounds and smells... see what there is to see... feel what there is to feel... you see a fire glowing near the mouth of the cave... and as you move towards it you hear the crackling of the flames and feel its warmth... and you know that other women have been here before you and have left this fire to welcome you... and you find that reassuring...

As you move towards the fire and the mouth of the cave you become aware of the pattern the flames make on the walls of the cave... flickering and dancing... creating shadows... and you notice they illuminate pictures on the walls of the cave... pictures painted in red... and you see that these pictures tell a story as you pass each of them in turn... a story of new beginnings and letting go... of birth and rebirth... of transformation and growth... and for a moment you feel awed by the wisdom and depth of experience all around you... then you remember that you yourself are part of this story... that this is your story... the journey portrayed on the walls of the cave is your journey... and you continue forward knowing you are seen and supported by all the women who have been here before you...

As you move towards the mouth of the cave... ready to emerge into what lies beyond... the fire suddenly rages up... bigger and wiser... filling the mouth of the cave... you stop... unsure of how you can go forward... and look back wondering if you can return that way... but where the staircase was there is now only smooth rock... you turn to face the fire again and you see between you and the fire is an animal... a guide on the journey... and whatever animal appears to you is right for you... and as you gaze into the animal's eyes you sense it is giving you courage... and you also know that the only way to go is through the fire at the mouth of the cave... and taking a deep breath you step forward... into the fire... and for a moment you think it will engulf you...

And you step forward... out of the cave now... into a sunny meadow... the breeze fresh on your face... and you feel a sense of triumph and freedom... and you also know that passing through the fire has changed you... that you have grown and transformed... and one day you will paint the stories on the wall to guide other women through the fire... you feel strong... and powerful... and beautiful... and reborn...

For a few moments you allow yourself to bask in those feelings... (pause here for a few moments).

And you can bring yourself back to your body and your breath now, ready to return to your waking life, knowing that you can bring these new feelings and new responses with you... and when you return you will return refreshed and alert.

Take a few more moments to enjoy this relaxation before you begin to wake up... feeling calm and refreshed... and you will begin to wake up as I count from one to five... fully refreshed... calm and alert... one... beginning to come up... two... becoming aware of the room around you... three... eyelids beginning to flicker... four... nearly there now... and five... OPEN YOUR EYES AND LOOK AROUND YOU, ALERT AND REFRESHED.

Resources/References

Labyrinth of Birth: Creating a Map, Meditations and Rituals for Your Childbearing Year – Pam England (Seven Gates Media, 2010)
www.positivebirthstories.com
www.positivebirthmovement.org
https://themandalajourney.com/about/birth-art/
www.birthingartbirthingheart.com

Chapter Two – How to Have a Happy Birth

The whole point of woman-centred birth is the knowledge that the woman is the birth power source. She may need and deserve help, but in essence she always had, currently has and will have the power.

Heather McCue

So you've started to change your birth narrative and harness your creativity; yet undoubtedly what most pregnant women looking at positive birth experiences want to know is how to actually have one. As mentioned in the Introduction, certain factors tend to be present for a positive birth. In this chapter we'll look at some of these in turn (a safe environment, a feeling of choice and control, a caring birth companion and effective and empowering techniques to manage sensation) and I'll share ways in which you can ensure these are present at your birth, regardless of what type of birth you have. One thing all of these factors have in common is they promote high levels of the hormone oxytocin.

During birth, keeping those oxytocin levels high is crucial. Although the interplay of hormones and neurotransmitters during birth is complex, at its most basic it comes down to this: birth needs oxytocin. Lots of it.

Oxytocin is a powerful hormone produced by the hypothalamus and secreted by the pituitary gland, which turns into a neurotransmitter in the brain. Known popularly, and quite appropriately, as the 'love hormone' oxytocin is the physiological process of falling in love and pair bonding, helping us to stay monogamous and committed to our partner. It is present when we smile, kiss and spend time with our loved ones. But its most crucial function is during reproduction. It is naturally released in high levels at birth, where it stimulates the uterus to contract, helps milk production and encourages mother and baby bonding.

Unfortunately, the medical model of birth is completely counterproductive to the release of oxytocin, and this has consequences for the natural progression of labour, which may as a result of inhibited oxytocin be longer, painful and more likely to result in complication and intervention. Breastfeeding may be more difficult, and physiological bonding between the mother and her baby interrupted. This can lead to far-reaching consequences, not the least of which is post-natal depression.

Why is a medicalised birth so inconducive to natural oxytocin production? There are two main reasons, the first of which has to do with our nervous system. High levels of oxytocin produce a positive feedback loop of a cocktail of hormones and neurotransmitters such as melatonin (which governs rest and relaxation), vasopressin (which has a part to play in bonding and connection) and endorphins (the body's natural high). This activates our parasympathetic nervous system, also known as our self-soothing system or the 'calm and connection' response. A medicalised birth, however, is more likely to leave us feeling stressed and anxious. This is the exact opposite of what we need as this activates our sympathetic nervous system, leading to high levels of adrenaline and cortisol – the 'stress hormone' – otherwise known as the fight-or-flight response. As one cannot be 'on' at the same time as the other, any stress or anxiety greatly inhibits the natural progression of labour.

Environment

The second reason the medical model of birth doesn't help the natural oxytocin release needed for a positive birth is because a hospital environment doesn't generally promote feelings of calm. The lists below make this apparent:

Oxytocin likes
- dim lights

- privacy
- calm
- familiar, homely surroundings
- loving touch
- warmth
- softness

Oxytocin doesn't like
- bright lights
- interruption
- pressure
- unfamiliar, clinical surroundings
- no touch or uncaring touch
- cold
- harshness

Given that your average hospital birth often involves a sterile and uncomfortable hospital room filled with rotating medical stuff routinely monitoring and examining you and it's understandable that oxytocin, which is also known as the 'shy' hormone, often beats a hasty retreat. For these reasons, many women desiring a gentler birth experience may want to consider a home birth.

Worried they're not safe? Think again. The 2011 Birthplace study in the UK found that for straightforward, uncomplicated pregnancies a home birth was as safe – and in some areas safer – as a hospital birth. Traditionally, women would always have given birth at home, often attended by female members of their own family. A home birth means you are in a safe, familiar setting and more likely to have continuity of care from your midwife or maternity nurse.

However, not all women will find the idea of a home birth the least anxiety-provoking option. Some studies show that first-time mothers in particular may feel more reassured knowing there is an obstetrician to hand; also women with older children running around or who are likely to fuss about the mess or be worrying about whether the laundry is folded may feel less distracted outside the home. In many countries in the West midwife-led birthing centres are now available which often marry the best of both environments, being close to hospital care if needed but also incorporating more relaxing environments, often complete with a birthing pool, birthing balls and plenty of privacy and warmth. Find out what resources and options are available in your area and remember – you have a choice.

What if your choices are limited? For some, birthing at home may not be an option and there may be no birthing centre in your area. Women who are giving birth to twins or multiples or otherwise classified as high-risk may have a hospital birth as their only viable option. You still, particularly in the UK where you are legally entitled to have the birth you choose, have a choice but may well decide that you would prefer to be under medical care if, after doing your own research, you feel your risks are higher than average. That doesn't mean you can't have a calm birthing environment; it just means you may have to put a little more effort into creating it.

Tell your caregivers it's important for you to have a calm, safe environment and that you will be bringing a few things with you. Although redecorating and furnishing the room might be out of the question, there's no reason you can't get creative with cushions and blankets, a favourite shawl or beanbag – anything that feels comfortable and reminds you of home. Bring some relaxing music, a scented room spray and ask for the lights to be dimmed. These simple changes can go a long way in completely changing how you feel in the environment and the more relaxed and at home you feel, the more oxytocin you will naturally release.

Exercise – Your Portable Oxytocin Kit

Close your eyes, take a few deep breaths, and remind yourself of the last time you felt deeply relaxed, perhaps as you were pleasantly drifting off to a good night's sleep.

Remember the environment you were in, and imagine yourself back there. What was the temperature of the room like? What sounds, smells and colours were present that helped you to relax? Who was with you?

Take a few more deep breaths, then come back to the present and open your eyes. Ask yourself: how could you recreate that scene? How could you make it portable? Write a list of items you could take anywhere with you that reminds you of that relaxing environment. Your favourite purple blanket, a meditation CD, a bowl of rose potpourri, etc.

This is your portable oxytocin kit. Pack it into your hospital bag ready for your birth.

Choice and Control

A common theme that stands out in accounts of traumatic events, including birth traumas, is often not so much the circumstances and events themselves, but the *feelings of powerlessness*. Feeling disempowered, helpless, exposed, trapped and in extreme cases in fear of your own or a loved one's life is the single biggest predictor of Post-Traumatic Stress. Unfortunately, many women report feeling this way after a birth which didn't go according to plan or was far from what they expected.

Birth can be unpredictable. Although evidence-based studies show that medical intervention in birth all too often happens unnecessarily, there will always be times when intervention is genuinely called for. Placenta praevia, where the placenta lies low and blocks the cervix, is rare but does happen and inevitably results in a C-section. Premature births occur and certain conditions such as pre-eclampsia may lead to an induction. In these cases, women are more likely to feel victims of circumstance and no longer in control of what happens to them. Even in more routine births, due to unfriendly staff, busy hospital wards and lack of communication from caregivers, women may feel it is the medical staff in control of their labour, not them, and may be sadly misinformed or under-informed about their choices and rights. Under these circumstances, and often laid flat on a hospital bed and subject to repeated examinations, even the most routine medical birth can leave the woman feeling disempowered and possibly traumatised.

Sadly we can't always afford to change caregivers or hospitals but we can take responsibility for informing ourselves. Thanks to new, evidence-based research and the efforts of birth practitioners there is a wealth of information out there that will tell you what your doctors may not. The more armed with facts you are, the more aware you are of your choices and the more in control you will feel, regardless of what actually happens. Imagine the difference in feelings between the woman who is told she is taking too long to push and so agrees to forceps and an episiotomy because she feels she has no other option and her doctor is putting pressure on her, and the woman who, having done her research, calmly asks for a little more time and for the doctor to leave the room, changes position and pushes her baby out with the help of her midwife and birth partner. Or perhaps intervention is needed, but she discusses her options with the doctor and makes a choice based on her own knowledge and intuition. Either way, she has retained some choice and control and is more likely to see her experience as being positive overall.

Regarding the Internet: social media and Mumsnet aren't reliable sources of information! Do your research wisely and seek out the experts. I've tried to give a wealth of unbiased and reliable resources in this book, so they would be a good place to start. Of course, I could have written a much bigger book and incorporated all of this information, complete with data and statistics, but that would have made it a less than enjoyable read, and besides, we're talking about the importance of choice and control here. Doing your own fact-finding (with a little guidance) is both empowering and enables you to compare arguments and make up your own mind. I fully believe that if you put a little trust in your own intuition, you will be guided towards what you need to know.

Speaking of which... You have a legal right to know what is happening with your medical care and to have any decisions fully discussed with you and be given all the available information. This is known as 'informed consent'. In other words medical staff should not seek to gain your consent for a procedure without having first fully informed you of the risks and benefits. Another phrase – and one I prefer – is 'informed choice', meaning you are making the final decision based on the most up-to-date information to hand. In other words, the informed consent process means you may choose *not* to give consent, and you have the right to have that choice respected, and to be offered all other viable alternatives.

For informed consent to be valid it has to be freely and voluntarily given and you must be seen to be competent to make your own decisions; so you have the right to not be coerced into anything while under emotional distress. Of course, the midst of labour is not the time when you are focused on making objective decisions, which is why a birth plan is recommended, as well as a supportive birth partner that can advocate for you (see below). You are legally entitled to be made aware of all and any risks of any procedure as well as the benefits and alternatives, to be given time to discuss the options with your partner and have all your questions answered. Medical staff are often overworked and understaffed, and as a result may not always be appreciative of your rights in this area. You may even feel as though you're being a nuisance or worried about questioning those who give the impression of having authority, but remember: this is your birth and your baby and it will have far-reaching effects for you both. Informed consent isn't just a sop to women to make them feel better; not only can the process reduce the likelihood of stress and trauma but also the likelihood of medical error and recovery time, making for a win-win outcome.

Trying to remember all the dos and don'ts when you're heavily pregnant or even giving birth can feel like a lot of pressure at times. If you're faced with a choice about intervention or anything else, a good way to remember all the things you might want to ask is with the acronym BRAINS:

B for 'benefits'. What are the benefits of this procedure?

R for 'risk'. What are the risks?

A for 'alternatives'. What are they and how do they compare with the procedure being offered?

I is for 'instinct'. What is yours telling you?

N is for 'nothing'. Is it possible to do nothing at this time? (For example, if you are offered an induction at 40 weeks as a precaution and the baby seems perfectly healthy you may wish to just wait for a while.)

S is for 'smile'. Stressed medical staff appreciate a friendly face and you're more likely to get the same back! Smiling also instantly gives you and everyone in the vicinity an oxytocin boost.

Being armed with information beforehand is always a good idea to help you take back control of your birth, as well as empowering you with knowledge prior to talking to your care providers. A good place to get objective and up-to-date information in the UK is AIMS (Association for Improving Maternity Services). AIMS was set up by Sally Willington after she went public about her distressing experience of clinical antenatal and birth practices and was contacted by hundreds of women with similar experiences. AIMS now publishes a well-respected quarterly journal, provides up-to-date information and resources, and numbers midwives, doctors and researchers among its members. Another good reference is the NICE (National Institute for Health and Care Excellence) guidelines around maternity care. Don't be afraid to quote these if you feel your midwife or doctor isn't following their standards. Globally and particularly in the US, Evidence Based Birth aims to put current evidence around maternity care – usually left languishing in academic journals for years before there's even a whisper of it being implemented in practice – into the hands of the general public.

Worried that you can't possibly 'tell the experts'? Unfortunately, for various reasons, evidence-based care is slow to happen, taking twenty years on average to become routine. So if you take steps to get up to date with current research, you may well be aware of things that your midwife or doctor isn't.

On that note, it's important to remember that your midwife, consultant or obstetrician isn't 'the enemy'. Yes, there are obnoxious and ill-motivated people in all walks of life, but the majority of nurses, midwives and medical staff are genuinely caring and hard-working people. Unfortunately – particularly within the British National Health Service – they are often overworked and under-appreciated and are operating within a medicalised structure that doesn't give much room for compassionate, hands-on care. Also, consultants and obstetricians and sometimes midwives working primarily in maternity wards often genuinely believe birth is inherently dangerous and requires medical intervention, because that is what they have been taught. Obstetricians in particular have most likely never seen anything else, because they don't get called in to the undisturbed, uncomplicated births. Fear of litigation also often drives the rush to intervention. In most cases, medical negligence is more likely to be proven if nothing rather than something is done. It's not hard to see why a hospital-based, clinical delivery isn't often conducive to a positive birth: such a fear-based environment is at odds with everything needed for oxytocin production and a feeling of having choice and being in control.

That's why it's crucial that you, or your birth partner as your advocate, speak up about what you want and need. This can feel scary; many of us suffer from 'white-coat syndrome', a proven phenomenon where we are more likely to capitulate because of perceived expertise and authority. Remember: YOU are the expert here, in terms of what your body wants and needs to birth.

Here are some tips for expressing your needs to medical caregivers, always bearing in mind the 'S' of 'BRAINS':

- If you feel you are being pressured into something you're not sure about because you've been labelled 'high risk' ask what the actual absolute risks are in terms of real life percentages and tell them you need time to think about them – then contact an organisation such as AIMS or Evidence Based Birth to get up-to-date advice.
- If medical staff are talking over your head, speak up! Ask them to explain to you what they are talking about and how it affects you.
- If you feel they are acting without having read your birth plan, ask if they have read it, and if not request that they do so.
- If you're being told you can't have what you want (for example a home birth) explain how important this is to you and ask what their reasons are for discouraging you. Ask about your options, and make it clear you will seek alternative care if they do not do their best to accommodate you.

Remember: do your research and stick to your guns about what is important to you. Just smile and be polite about it!

Exercise – A New Approach to Your Birth Plan

There are a lot of templates around for writing a birth plan, and some hospitals and birthing centres will make these available as part of your maternity notes. However, you may find these are too 'one size fits all'. Unfortunately, although writing out a 1500-word birth plan covering all your wishes, hopes and dreams may be a positive exercise for you, you may find caregivers have little time to read it through thoroughly, particularly on a busy maternity ward (if you're having a home birth this won't be as much of an issue, so write away). For this reason, I would personally advise making a birth plan that is little more than a bullet pointed list of what you do want and what you definitely don't want. That way, your midwife or obstetrician can see your preferences at a glance. Don't worry about being brusque; brevity will most likely be appreciated. If you're struggling with how to organise all your thoughts, fears and wishes into a coherent plan, try the following steps:

- *Review your answers to the journalling questions in the last chapter.*
- *Look at your vision board, or imagine what your perfect birth would look like. What do you need for this to happen?*
- *Talk to your birth partner/s, do your research and trust your instincts.*
- *Think about the things that are most important to you and create a list of 'dos', for example: at least an hour of immediate and undisturbed skin-to-skin contact with my baby, or your birth partner to be present at all times.*
- *Think about the things that would be definite negatives for you and create a list, for example: no vaginal examinations unless strictly necessary; no episiotomy. Remember, you don't need to justify or explain yourself on your birth plan.*
- *Put these together and you've got your birth plan.*
- *Make copies: one for yourself, one to keep with your*

maternity notes, one to give to caregivers at the birth and one for each birth partner.

Birth Companions

The UK Royal College of Midwives recently published an evidence-based report on the role of birth partners, concluding that women should be allowed the birth partners of their choice and companionship throughout the entire birth, as this promotes positive outcomes and maternal well-being. Recent research into the effects of having a doula present (also known as a professional or traditional birth attendant, or even in other cultures as a lay midwife) show that having a doula can reduce the need for intervention and even additional pain relief by fifty per cent. A supportive and loving birth companion provides emotional support and therefore raises oxytocin. They can also act as an advocate with the mother's permission.

More often than not, the mother's partner is the birth companion. This can lead to a deep bond between the partners, particularly if the baby's father is the partner and is loving and tactile during the birth (massage, hair stroking and kissing are all great ways to give oxytocin a boost), and also engages in holding the baby afterwards. However, many men feel daunted and unsure of what is expected of them. Men at birth is a relatively new phenomenon; traditionally birth was a woman's matter and birth attendants were usually female, often relatives of the mother. If you're planning on having your male partner present, take some time to sit and discuss both of your fears and expectations and your ideal vision for birth. Include him in your research and preparation, and ensure he knows your birth plan and why it is important for you. Encourage him to talk to other men who have attended positive births, and to watch and read positive birth stories. Relaxation and visualisation can also help; and there are resources available specifically for birth partners on the accompanying website for this book.

The crucial thing is that your birth partner/s are supportive and are *your* choice. So it's not a good idea to have anyone there who is likely to make you feel stressed and anxious or annoyed as that's the exact opposite of the soothing and connection you need! This can be difficult if you have a well-meaning but pushy female relative or in-law who expects or asks to be at the birth, but remember this is your moment, your baby and that takes precedent over emotional guilt trips. Just say a polite 'thank you, but no'.

Doulas or hired birth companions are becoming more and more popular in the West as the importance of a supportive, female birth companion is recognised. Once, a midwife would see the same woman antenatally, during birth and postnatally, and provide emotional support as much as medical care. However, medicalisation of birth has changed the role of the midwife to a more clinical caregiver. Recent legislation in the UK and other areas has also made it next to impossible to hire an independent midwife to fulfil a more traditional role. Doulas are filling the gap. A doula may be hired by couples as an extra support and pair of hands, perhaps to fill the roles the partner feels unsure of. For example, a male partner may feel more confident doing the practical stuff and advocating, while a doula is employed for emotional support and nurturing, or vice versa.

Doulas may also be hired by women without partners who are able or willing to be present, or as an extra birth companion so the woman feels as supported as possible, or as an attendant at a home birth. In fact, in any situation where a woman wants one! The original meaning of the word 'doula' in Greek is 'servant' and doulas often describe their role as 'mothering the mother'. Many people ask me when I tell them I do doula work, 'What does a doula do?' and the best answer is probably, 'Whatever the mother needs.' A doula is not there as a health practitioner or to give clinical advice but to support and nurture the mother through a precious, powerful and vulnerable time. Most doulas will have a 'toolkit' of recipes, sensation management tips, resources and skills to adapt to individual needs.

Some points to consider if you are thinking of hiring a doula include:

- Are you looking for practical help (for example providing food or looking after older children at a home birth) or emotional support? Try making a checklist.
- Who is available in your local area? A local doula is best if you want them to be there at your birth at a moment's notice.
- Interview. If you have a few doulas available in your local area, meet with them in turn (most doulas expect and will be fine with this) and find out if their skill set best matches your checklist.
- Do you want a doula for the birth, postnatally, or both? Postnatal doulas can offer practical and emotional support in those precious first few months, help with breastfeeding, weaning, looking after older children and possibly even housework. More about postnatal doulas in the next section.
- Cost. Depending on where you live or how much support you need, a doula can be costly (although in truth many people will spend just as much on a state-of-the-art buggy so sometimes it comes down to prioritising). If you're struggling, Doula UK run a limited Access Fund for people in need and you can also get friends and family to buy gift vouchers to put towards the cost. Some doulas in training will do low cost work in exchange for the experience and there are non-profit organisations available in some areas.

Managing the Sensations

Birth doesn't have to hurt. Often, when I say that to women

whose only experiences or knowledge about birth have involved high levels of intervention and pain relief, they look shocked, disbelieving and, often, a little bit hopeful. 'Really?' Yes, really.

Of course, pain is very subjective; what feels excruciating to one person may be nothing at all to another, so it's impossible and unethical to promise any woman that it won't hurt at all. On that note, it's just as unethical and unrealistic to try and convince a woman that her birth will be agonising and she will need to accept every form of pain relief going. We just don't know. What researchers do know, however, is that women having calm, undisturbed births where they feel loved and supported, and that they have choice and control, experience less pain. Some women experience no pain. A minority of women even report having orgasms during birth! Many women report feelings of intense euphoria either during or after birth.

So why the excruciating reputation? As explored above, the 'norm' in most of the West is for a medicalised birth in a clinical environment. This leads to more stress and less oxytocin. Not only do we need oxytocin for our bodies' natural painkillers (endorphins) to be released, but stress (fear) also leads to tension, which leads to pain. This is known as the fear-tension-pain cycle. Also, the more tense we are during birth, the less efficient our contractions. Relaxation, warmth and softness are needed for the cervix to dilate and for the baby to move down the birth canal.

Our belief affects our experience. You may have heard of the 'placebo' effect, whereby people who believe they have been given medicine feel better and even physically heal, even though the 'medicine' they have been given contains no active ingredients. Scientists have also documented the 'nocebo' effect which works on the same principle but in the opposite direction: people given medicine or painkillers without their knowledge don't feel better, because they don't expect to. In some cases they may even feel worse! Our beliefs may play a big part – if not the main part – in shaping our reality. The *National Geographic* magazine ran a piece in its December 2016 issue about the power of belief, reporting how unconscious cues in our environment can trigger our physiological responses. Our society primes us to expect pain in birth. Exposing ourselves to a different narrative, as described in Chapter One, changing our environment, feeling in control and being surrounded by supportive partners all help to ease fear and change our expectations, as well as help to boost oxytocin and endorphins on a physiological level.

Of course, there are many alternatives available to help you manage the sensations of birth which, painful or not, are usually intense. As with everything else, do a little research and make your choices based on what's best for you and your baby. Some women will sail through birth with little more than a few position changes and breathing exercises, some may not. Putting unnecessary pressure on yourself that you must have a wholly natural birth may only increase stress. So before we look at some tried and tested holistic ways to manage birth sensations, let's have a look at some of the pros and cons of medical pain relief and why you might choose it alongside other methods. (It doesn't have to be either/or. I've worked with women who have used, for example, a combination of a birthing pool, hypnobirthing and gas and air and been very satisfied with their experience.)

As birth progresses and contractions become closer together, some women may feel the need for stronger relief. The most common time for a birthing woman to suddenly shout for medical management of sensation is during the transition from first to second stage labour, when the cervix is nearly fully dilated. This is because contractions are at their most intense and the body naturally produces a sudden surge of adrenalin to give energy for the actual delivery. Transition doesn't usually last very long, and in my experience when women know this and see it as a sign their baby is soon arriving, it can become an exciting rather than stressful period of birth, or even barely noticed. Unfortunately, typical antenatal classes don't fully explain the rhythms of labour, and so a woman experiencing transition without knowing what is happening may become tense and scared – leading, of course, to much more pain. Because at transition it is too late for an epidural or opiates these are often offered earlier on, which further sets up the expectation of pain. As in my own experience, many women report how their birth sensations were more than manageable until medical staff started talking about pain relief, therefore anticipating the need for it. If you wish you can put on your birth plan that you don't want to be offered pain relief; if you want it you will ask for it. This leaves you with the choice.

The three most common forms of pain relief offered by medical staff are:

- Epidurals. Anaesthetic is administered via a large needle in the back. Although this offers complete lack of any sensation, it also involves being immobile, monitored almost continuously, and at much higher risk of intervention such as forceps or an emergency C-section during delivery as you are in a prone position and often unable to feel the sensation of pushing. There is an option available in some hospitals now for a partial epidural where a 'baseline' of anaesthetic is delivered and a button given for the woman to push to release more if needed, allowing for some control over the level of numbness. A catheter is often also needed with an epidural as you will not be able to feel the need to urinate. Epidurals are therefore not the best option for women who want to be able to move around, feel their labour progressing and reduce the risk of intervention, or for women who find medical procedures stressful. Epidurals don't always work and after-effects may include loss of bladder control, chronic backache and an acute headache. Epidurals are often routinely given during an induction by syntocinon drip as the effect of the syntocinon can produce unnaturally strong contractions. The 'fake oxytocin' administered only stimulates contractions, it doesn't activate the calm and connection response or encourage endorphin release. There is ongoing research into possible negative long-term effects of this drug during labour, though at the time of writing there are not yet any conclusive results.

- Opiates. Pethidine, diamorphine or similar may be offered. Their effects on contraction sensation is variable, and side effects include nausea and difficulties in baby's breathing at birth. There is also some debate about the possible long-term effects on the baby of being given these drugs, as they certainly would be considered dangerous during pregnancy. However, they are a less immobilising choice than an epidural, allowing for freedom of movement.

- Entonox (gas and air). There are no known side effects of this, other than nausea in some women, and it can be made available at a home birth or with a birthing pool etc. It can cause a tendency to tighten the jaw due to the way it is administered, which can cause tension in the pelvis, so if you opt for this try to make a conscious effort to relax your lower face in between puffs! Gas and air can also be used during vaginal examinations or injections to help the mother relax if she finds these stressful. Alternatively self-hypnosis and mindfulness techniques such as the one below and at www.happybirthhappybaby.co.uk can help with interventions like this as well as with contractions.

It's also worth remembering that no matter what your experience of contractions, over two-thirds of your labour is naturally designed to be completely pain-free! The average contraction wave lasts a minute and a half, with two minutes in between. In between contractions you can rest, hug your partner, laugh with your birth companion, practise meditation or visualisation, walk – or dance – around, have a drink or snack, the choice is yours. Transition is likely to be the only time when contractions seem never-ending, and thankfully this soon gives way to 'second-stage' labour or pushing. Most women having a relatively natural birth report second stage as, although intense, also something of a relief, where the body 'just takes over'.

If you are expecting twins or more, don't think that you have to do the whole thing all over again! The cervix only needs to dilate once, so you will only have one overall labour and transition stage; it is only the pushing and emerging stage that needs to be repeated. Contrary to popular opinion, therefore, a twin or multiple birth does not automatically mean more pain.

Mindfulness has become the new buzzword of the twenty-first century after the numerous research conducted into its positive therapeutic outcomes for everything from depression and anxiety to pain management. Originally an ancient meditation technique found in all the world's major spiritual traditions but particularly in its present form in Buddhism, mindfulness is incorporated into many third-wave behaviour therapies such as Mindfulness-Based Cognitive Therapy, Dialectical Behaviour Therapy, and Compassion Focused Therapy. As I will explore in a forthcoming book, these are particularly helpful in treating postnatal depression and anxiety. With mindfulness being used in everything from psychology to colouring books, mindful birthing wasn't far behind, and the gentle breathing techniques have been shown to be more effective at aiding labour than the traditional 'hold your breath and tuck your chin into your chest', which only exacerbates tension and tires both the mother and her baby. In its essence, mindfulness is simply bringing the focus to the present moment, using the breath, a sound, or current sensation. Deceptively simple, it can be a great aid in birth because of its proven use in decreasing stress and anxiety, managing pain and promoting the calm and connection and self-soothing responses (oxytocin again!). Practise the techniques below until they become familiar, and you may find them a great help during pregnancy, birth and beyond.

Exercise – Mindfulness of Sensations

Take a few deep breaths, closing your eyes and turning your intention inwards. Bring your awareness to your breath as it moves in and out... following it down your airways, into your lungs, aware of the rise and fall of your chest and diaphragm... After a few breaths, bring your attention down your body, from the crown of your head to the soles of your feet... Note where there is any stiffness, any uncomfortableness, any tension, and bring your awareness here... still breathing deeply and slowly... allow yourself to be aware of this sensation without attempting to change it or fight against it... simply accept... if you feel yourself struggling with it or getting caught up in your thoughts, simply bring your attention back to your breath, and then back to the sensation... simply accepting it is there without judging it... take your breath, still calm and slow, into the sensation... feel your breath soften and soothe... soften and soothe... allowing the sensation to melt away along with your exhale... continue this way for as long as it feels good... open your eyes and stretch your body... how does it feel now?

Exercise – Centring Wave

(You may like to do this immediately after either the exercise above or the mindfulness meditation in Chapter One. It's also a good idea to practise this when you're getting Braxton Hicks.)

Breathe in and out slowly and deeply, turning your attention to any sensations in your body. Make your exhale a little longer than your inhale.

As you inhale, say to yourself, 'I breathe in peace.'

As you exhale, tell yourself, 'I let go of any tension.'

Continue for a few breaths, then reduce the mantra (but keep the breaths long), breathing in 'peace' and breathing out 'let go'. Keep doing this until your breath and the mantra seem to merge together and become fluid, like the rising and falling of a wave. Observe the rising and falling of your chest and belly. Feel your breath, your body and the words of the mantra as parts of a whole.

Hypnobirthing is currently in vogue as the sensation management technique of choice as women turn away from medical intervention towards taking charge of their own births; and for good reason. Despite the name, hypnobirthing isn't about being hypnotised into some strange trance state that will convince you you're not feeling anything. The 'trance' state described in hypnosis is something as natural to us as breathing, and we access it every time we daydream, become absorbed in a creative task or meditate. In this state we are deeply relaxed and our calming responses activated; we're also more in touch with our powerful subconscious mind and able to communicate positive messages for healing. In a nutshell, that's how hypnotherapy works. Hypnobirthing is similar in that it teaches women self-hypnosis, relaxation and visualisation techniques designed to help them get into a calm and deeply relaxed state. Hypnobirthers call this the 'birthing zone' but this isn't some hypnotically manufactured zone, but rather the oxytocin-rich and natural state of a birthing woman when labour is left to progress naturally. This is the 'liminal time' we spoke about in the first chapter. In short, hypnobirthing is a way of teaching our conscious mind to relax and get out of the way so our bodies can get on with doing what comes naturally. Hypnobirthing is recognised as drastically reducing the need for pain relief, and was popularised when British Princess Kate Middleton reportedly used it for the birth of Princess Charlotte.

To get a taste of how guided relaxation and visualisation can promote a positive and pain-free birth experience, try recording the following script and playing it back to yourself, or download it from the website.

Exercise – Birth Visualisation Script

Just get yourself comfortable now... and now let your eyes find something on that wall... some spot or corner or a small object... and let your eyes rest on that point while you listen to the sound of my voice... hold your eyes open... and just look at that spot or that point... for a few moments... keep focusing on that spot... and your eyelids become heavy... heavier and heavier... blinking more and more... you can feel those eyelids becoming so heavy... but you just keep them open now... they may begin to water... that's okay... just keep them open... keep focusing... heavier and heavier... even though you want to close them you can keep them open for a few moments longer... and now close your eyes down... and as you close your eyes down you feel a wave of relaxation sweep through your entire body...

Now just focus on your breathing... breathing deeply... as you become so very deeply relaxed... breathing in... and breathing out... feeling your lungs and stomach expand as you breathe in... and your body relax so very deeply as you breathe out... relaxing more and more...

And now become aware of the quality of that relaxation... and imagine that relaxation spreading through the whole of your body... sweeping down from the top of your head to the tips of your toes... like a wave of relaxation... letting go... let go and relax every muscle in your body... that's right... really feel that relaxation from the crown of your head to the tips of your toes... feel how very good it feels to be this deeply relaxed...

And as deep as you are now... you can go ten times deeper. In a moment I am going to ask you to open your eyes... and then when you close them again you will go ten times deeper... so very deeply relaxed... relaxed in body and mind...

Now you may find it difficult to open your eyes... but you are able to open them a bit... so open them a bit now... and then allow them to close and go ten times deeper... just like that.

And as relaxed as you are now... you can actually become ten times more relaxed... relaxed in body and mind... so you can open your eyes a second time and you might be able to open them a little and then as those eyelids come down you feel yourself going ten times deeper again...

And now do this for a third time... and as those eyes shut tight... you will go even deeper... ten times deeper...

And you can just take a few moments now to enjoy how very deeply relaxed you are in body and mind...

When you are ready I want you to imagine... in as much detail as is right for you now... a beautiful spiral staircase that takes you down to a special place... a safe place that is just for you... maybe the staircase has an ornate textured handrail, or maybe it is more plain and smooth, whatever is right for you now... either way it feels inviting to you and you go down... a step at a time... as I count from ten to one... and as I do so you can imagine yourself going down... a step at a time... going deeper and deeper... ten... nine... eight... see yourself going down... seven... six... hear your footsteps on the stairs, feel the stairs beneath your feet, and imagine yourself going deeper still... five... four... three... two... one... you step down and you can find yourself in your special place... and you can explore and take in all of the wonderful things there are to experience... all of the sights and sounds and smells... see what there is to see... feel what there is to feel... and just for a few moments take in all of the details of your special place... knowing that this safe place is just for you and you can return here whenever you choose...

Bring your attention now to your baby... knowing that as you are so very deeply relaxed so is your baby... And just as you are in your safe space so is your baby... deeply relaxed and calm inside you... safe and protected... and I would like you to imagine now that you are building a bubble around you both... a bubble that will keep you safe from worry... safe from fear... safe from stress... build this bubble around you... and see its colour... it can be any colour you choose... as bright or as soft as you like... and stretch out your arms and feel the texture of this bubble all around you... it can be any texture you like... any tone... soft and smooth... or some other texture... this is your bubble and you can choose to create it however you wish now... and take a few minutes to feel and see this bubble around you... knowing that it keeps you and your baby safe and protected and able to deal with anything... and worries just bounce off this bubble and away... they just bounce off and away... shielding you from worry and stress... and you know that you are safe inside this bubble and that you can choose to recreate this bubble in your waking life any time you choose... any time you are going into a situation you may find stressful you can imagine this bubble around you... keeping you safe... it is yours to use any time you wish... send love to your baby... feel this love wrapping around your baby just like the bubble... safe and calm...

Now imagine yourself at the birth... see yourself there with loving and supportive birth partners... excited about the arrival of your baby... greeting your baby with love and calm... see yourself in your perfect birthing environment... create around you and your baby all the things you need to feel calm and relaxed... safe and protected... know that everything will happen in just the right time... in just the right way... your body and your baby know exactly what to do... and you are calm and relaxed... safe and protected... feeling your body soften and relax... your womb soften and open... allowing your baby to move down... move out... calm and relaxed... safe and protected... see yourself knowing just what to do... your body knows instinctively how to birth your baby and you can just relax and let it happen... excited to meet your baby... welcoming your baby with love... surrounded with love and support... feel how each sensation in your body brings your baby closer and closer to you... welcoming your baby with love... calm

*and relaxed... imagine now you have your baby in your arms...
greeting your baby... feel how very good that feels... feel that love
and joy for your baby sweeping through your entire body... and take
a few moments to just stay with that feeling... calm and relaxed...
safe and protected... welcoming your baby with love...*

*And you can bring yourself back to your safe place now, ready
to return to your waking life, knowing that you can bring these new
feelings and new responses with you... and when you return you
will return refreshed and alert.*

*Take a few more moments to enjoy your special place before you
begin to wake up... feeling calm and refreshed... and you will begin
to wake up as I count from one to five... fully refreshed... calm and
alert... one... beginning to come up... two... becoming aware of the
room around you... three... eyelids beginning to flicker... four...
nearly there now... and five... OPEN YOUR EYES AND LOOK
AROUND YOU, ALERT AND REFRESHED.*

To really get to grips with hypnobirthing I would suggest taking
a class. There are different schools of hypnobirthing, of which the
Mongan Method, set up by Marie Mongan, is perhaps the most
famous, but they are all based on the same principles of calm,
relaxation, optimum physiological conditions and self-efficacy
(in other words 'you can do it!'). My own personal favourite is
Mindful Mamma, set up by psychologist and doula Mia Scotland
and clinical hypnotherapist and doula Sophie Fletcher, the author
of the bestselling *Mindful Hypnobirthing*. Mindful Mamma blends
the latest in research into the psychology and physiology of birth
with hypnobirthing and mindfulness techniques and has become
recognised and recommended by birth workers, midwives and
doctors. Another reason I love their approach is the way the class
also focuses on the role of the birth partner and how they can help
the woman with the techniques and also use the principles to keep
themselves calm and relaxed. I spoke to Sophie, who trained me in
hypnobirthing, about the origins of Mindful Mamma:

I founded Mindful Mamma in 2008. I really felt there was a need for a class that combined mindfulness with hypnosis. These techniques help you to soothe your mind, manage contractions and get into your birthing zone. They help you to manage both emotional and physical sensations during your baby's birth, and used during pregnancy can also reduce any perinatal stress or anxiety. This is important for your baby as studies now show babies can feel their mothers' stress in the womb and this can have an impact on the neurological development of your baby's brain. So even if you're intending to have a caesarean birth, hypnosis and mindfulness can be of great benefit.

Natural remedies such as homeopathic and herbal remedies and essential oils can also be used to promote calm and muscle relaxation in birth, but please do seek out an experienced and well qualified practitioner who specialises in pregnancy and birth, as some herbs and oils are contraindicated and can even be toxic in heavy doses.

Water births have become enduringly popular in the last few decades. According to birth expert Michel Odent women in labour are naturally drawn to water. Given that being immersed in water during birth is a safe and low cost way to relax, get into the birthing zone and ease sensation, it would seem that this instinctive gravitation towards water is for very good reason. Water birth advocates claim that this way of birthing both eases contractions (in much the same way as relaxing into a warm bath eases menstrual cramps) and boosts oxytocin. There are also claims, however, that getting into the water in early labour may slow down the progress of labour, but Waterbirth International claim the opposite is true, which would seem to make sense in light of what we know about relaxation and oxytocin helping labour along. Studies seem to be inconclusive. Either way, there are many documented benefits to a water birth, including: allowing for a private enclosed space for the mother, conservation of energy, ease of aches and pains, the feeling of buoyancy relieves heaviness and gives more freedom of movement, and rates of intervention, drugs and perineal trauma are greatly reduced. Such is the widespread acceptance of water births that most birthing centres will have a birth pool and they can be easily hired for home births. Even a great deal of consultant-led birthing wards have at least one birthing pool or at the very least access to a nice big bath, so do ask your providers what's available in your area. You can also relax in water at home in early labour before moving to the birthing suite or ward. During my last birth, although I didn't get access to the birthing pool as I'd originally wanted, I spent quite a few hours in the bathroom with my husband, floating in one of the deep, big baths they had available, listening to my hypnobirthing tracks and enjoying the privacy. I felt very between worlds, in that liminal space we spoke about earlier, and incredibly in tune with my body and baby, so I can certainly recommend the use of water during birth.

Movement is also important. The medical model has women lying on their backs, possibly with feet in stirrups. As well as increasing the chances of emotional trauma due to the woman feeling exposed, helpless and passive in her own birthing role, this is physiologically the least efficient way to birth. As a result this can cause unnecessary pain. Traditionally women birthed kneeling, squatting, on all fours or standing up hanging on to a rope or even branch overhead. These positions allow for easier passage of the baby down the birth canal, opening the pelvis and allowing gravity to help. Lying on the back acts against gravity and puts the pelvis at totally the wrong angle. So why did birthing on the back become the norm? Quite simply, it made it easier for medical professionals to intervene. It wasn't that long ago, and in fact still happens in many countries, that the woman would be strapped down so she didn't obstruct the obstetrician in any way.

Thankfully in recent years medical professionals have become aware of the need to allow women freedom of movement in birth, although this is hampered if you are in a consultant-led unit and are expected to have continuous monitoring (you can decline this), and certainly if you are having an epidural. Many birthing suites or midwife-led units will have birthing balls or birthing stools to hand or you can bring your own.

Of course there is no one 'correct' position to give birth in; it all depends on what feels right for you and your body. A birthing woman who is allowed unrestricted movement will instinctively move into the positions that feel right for her at different stages in the labour. The mindfulness of sensations movement above will help you feel in tune with your body and its needs in the moment.

Movement during the early stages of labour can be very effective in reducing uncomfortableness or cramping, and also helps labour progress. Tune into your body, perhaps using the breathing techniques or self-hypnosis to get into the 'birthing zone' and allow your body to move in whichever way it feels it needs to. Your birth partner can help you in this by supporting you – particularly if you are in a squatting position later on in labour – or massaging your hips, lower back and thighs, or you can link your arms around their neck and let them take some of your weight. Try circling your hips or moving them in figures of eight, much as if you were belly dancing. In fact, belly dancing originated as a birth aid! Birthlight in the UK offer classes in 'yoga dance' which fuses traditional ethnic dances with maternity yoga to create a delicious fusion of movement, yoga and traditional practices which will help prepare you for labour and learn some moves you may like to use during birth. You can find their videos online (see Resources). For a more intuitive and less structured approach, try the exercise below when you are having aches and pains in late pregnancy or Braxton Hicks (commonly referred to as 'practice contractions') to discover how your body might want to move when you are in labour.

Exercise – Birth Dance

(You may like to practise the mindfulness of sensations exercise above before going straight into this exercise.)

Stand or kneel, or get on to all fours if this feels right for you. Bring your attention to your body and your breath... feel your breath circulating around your body... your blood flowing through you... your cells alive... your breath moving gently through you... and begin to sway your body gently in rhythm with your breath... however feels right for you... connect your movement with your breath...

Begin to sway your hips and lower back a little faster... a little deeper... whatever feels good... you may like to do figures of eight... move in whatever way your body wants to move... add sound if you wish... humming or singing...

Let your body take over... however it wishes to move... lift your arms... bend your knees... whatever feels good to you and your baby... listen to the messages your body is sending you... you may need to slow down... just rocking gently... listen to the wisdom of your body.

Resources/References

The Oxytocin Factor – Kerstin Uvnas-Moberg (Pinter & Martin, 2011)

http://www.aims.org.uk

Ina May's Guide to Childbirth – Ina May Gaskin (Bantam, 2003)

www.evidencebasedbirth.com

http://www.sarawickham.com/articles/

http://redtentdoulas.co.uk/

https://doula.org.uk/doula-access-fund/

https://www.dona.org/what-is-a-doula/

Gentle Birth Choices: A Guide to Making Informed Decisions –

Barbara Harper, RN (Healing Arts Press, 2005)
Mindful Hypnobirthing – Sophie Fletcher (Vermilion, 2014)
www.mindfulmamma.co.uk
https://us.hypnobirthing.com/
http://waterbirth.org
http://birthlight.com/page/birthlight-yoga-dance-for-pregnancy
Birth & Sex – Sheila Kitzinger (Pinter & Martin, 2013)

Chapter Three – When Birth Becomes a Challenge

Giving birth should be your greatest achievement, not your greatest fear.
Jane Weideman

I believe a woman-centred birth is possible in all situations if attention is given to the factors discussed in the previous two chapters; however, there are situations which can make a positive birth seem harder to obtain. In this chapter we will look at two of the major interventions – induction and Caesarean – and how to navigate them, and previous experiences that may cause extra anxiety around birth – namely, previous birth trauma, previous sexual abuse, and previous pregnancy loss.

It might seem strange to include these latter topics in a book about happy birth, but the fact is that many women will have had these experiences, and failure to address them can leave them feeling that an empowered birth experience is not possible for them. This is far from the case. Using the principles explored in this book can transform *any* birth, and by discussing and exploring any extra support needs, the woman is empowered to do so. Having suffered both trauma and pregnancy loss, I know this is to be true on a personal as well as a therapeutic level. That being said, if you feel like this chapter or parts of it may be any way triggering or upsetting for you, please skip ahead and come back when you feel able. Because of this I have listed relevant resources at the end of each section rather than the end of the chapter.

Inductions

Artificial induction of labour can save lives when mother and baby are at risk, for example in the case of infection or conditions such as pre-eclampsia. They also offer women in some high-risk situations an alternative to C-sections if they have their heart set on a vaginal delivery.

Clinical guidelines in most Western countries state that inductions without medical emergency are largely unnecessary – 'going over' due dates without any other complications or indications of distress is not a clinical reason for an induction. After 41 weeks, however, risks do slightly rise, particularly in a woman over her early thirties, though it is important to remember that risks do remain low overall. They can vary by country, so ask your caregiver for an accurate breakdown.

If you are having twins, you are likely to be offered an induction before 38 weeks, as this is when risks increase. The majority of twins or multiples are born naturally before 38 weeks, so this is considered 'term' for a multiple pregnancy.

To give yourself a clearer picture, ask what the absolute rather than the relative risk is for your personal situation. For example, in layman's terms a relative risk would be 'double the risk' which sounds very frightening, but if the original risk in a given situation was 0.01% then even doubled – 0.02% – the risk is actually very small. Knowing absolute risks will help you make an informed choice, as only you know how much risk is too much for your peace of mind. Most places will offer you regular, even daily, monitoring if you don't want an induction but do want to be reassured that your baby is calm and happy.

Although due dates are set at 40 weeks, a single pregnancy cannot accurately be classed as 'term' until 42 weeks. The World Health Organization doesn't class a pregnancy as prolonged until it has gone past 42 weeks. Only around 5% of babies arrive on their 'due date'. Up to 90% of babies will arrive before 42 weeks. The modern preoccupation with due dates is counter-intuitive to the natural unfolding of pregnancy and birth. Your baby doesn't know its due date! Not to mention the fact that dates can never be entirely accurate. Some women prefer to refer to their 'due month' as opposed to getting hung up on a specific date.

Your baby and your body communicate with each other through a complex chain of physiological factors, and it is believed by foetal development researchers that only when your baby is fully developed and ready to be born will your body go into labour. Your baby's lung development is key here. Babies born early are therefore at high risk for respiratory issues (the risk generally being higher the earlier the baby is). If you haven't gone into labour by your due date, it is likely to be because your baby isn't fully ready to be born. Induction also carries greater risk of uterine rupture and increases the likelihood of assisted delivery or an emergency Caesarean – a classic case of intervention leading to intervention. There is also research being done into the use of synthetic oxytocin and its long-term effects on mother and baby.

Despite all of this, induction rates across the US, UK, Australia and Canada are approximately 25%. Most of these will be before 42 weeks, and a vast proportion of these will occur purely because they are 'overdue'.

If you are offered an induction, or feel pressured into having one, remember to use BRAINS, and get all the information you need to make an informed choice. Watch and read positive birth stories of women who waited to go into spontaneous labour.

Induction may be necessary in some cases or in others it may be your choice. As I stated in the Introduction, I have had two, and still had overall positive and empowering birth experiences that I remember with joy. It's about weighing up the risks and benefits, and doing what is right for you. Even if your choices are restricted, you can still choose a positive mindset.

So how to make an induced birth a calmer and more empowering experience? You will be on a hospital ward, but you can still ask for a birthing pool or birth ball etc in the earlier stages (or do as I did and get in the bath). Use all of the oxytocin boosting techniques described in Chapter Two, which may also help counteract any negative effects of synthetic oxytocin. Consider hiring a doula. You may want to consider an epidural if you are on a synthetic oxytocin drip as they can make contractions painful. Many women, however, do perfectly well with hypnobirthing with some gas and air, and not all induced labours are more painful; see my own experiences. If you do opt for an epidural, in most places you can now request a mobile epidural which will allow you to move around, and as it doesn't completely numb you, you don't lose the awareness of 'when to push', something that is common during a full spinal block and which contributes to further intervention. You can also ask for an epidural where you are given the initial dose of local anaesthesia and then have a button which allows you to be in control of whether to top it up or not, up to a certain amount. These epidurals allow more choice and control and so make the experience much more empowering for many women.

This is a good place to mention episiotomy, as induction may make these more likely. An episiotomy (known as 'cutting') is where a surgeon makes an incision to your perineum to allow more room for baby to come out or to allow for forceps or a ventouse. Although they may occasionally be necessary, they can be largely avoided and they were a definite no-no on my birth plan. Many women report both physical and psychological trauma after an episiotomy and they are usually more painful and take a lot longer to heal than if you tear naturally. Thankfully these are no longer nearly as common as they once were, although in some US states they are still performed as routine. Some women may opt for these as they are frightened of tearing, not realising their recovery time is likely to be a lot longer with an episiotomy. Tearing is never as common and nearly always not as bad as you think. I didn't even realise it had happened at my first birth until the midwife told me!

If you are worried about this, there are things you can do

to prepare the area and keep it supple and elastic, such as massaging it with a warm oil in the weeks before birth. This has been proven to reduce tearing.

Exercise – Prenatal Perineal Massage

Get comfortable, lying back on plenty of pillows, and relax, bending your knees and allowing them to gently fall open.

Warm a little oil in your hands. Olive oil will do in a pinch, or try grapeseed or jojoba or a specially blended oil for the purpose by a company such as motherlylove.co.uk.

Massage into the area using a firm but gentle circular rhythm. Imagine your vagina and perineum softening and opening as you do so.

Place your fingers up to 2 inches into the vagina and apply downwards pressure, moving around in a U shape. If you feel a little burning or tingling here, this is what it will feel like when your baby's head is crowning!

Finish with gentle strokes over the perineum, then cup your hand over the whole area and apply gentle pressure. You may like to imagine sending loving thoughts to the area.

Just remember; it's YOUR birth.

Resources/References

https://www.motherlylove.co.uk/product/perineum-massage-oil-perineal/

https://www.naturalbirthandbabycare.com/going-overdue-postdates-pregnancy/

https://pathways.nice.org.uk/pathways/induction-of-labour

Caesareans

When performed in a genuine emergency, Caesareans, like inductions, are life savers. Elective Caesareans may also be needed in the case of conditions such as placenta praevia, where the placenta covers the cervix and prevents delivery. There has been a worrying trend in the rise of unnecessary Caesarean sections in the last decade, however, especially in the US where nearly a third of all births are by C-section. An operation designed for specific circumstances is becoming all too routine, and recent research is discovering this may have knock-on effects for mother and baby. In this section we will focus on transforming the experience for the mother, and we will look at ways to make a C-section more natural for baby in the next chapter.

Because of the medicalisation of birth and the culture of fear that has grown up around it in the Western world, a Caesarean is often seen as the easiest option. However, with a longer recovery time (while trying to look after a newborn!) and increased risk of infection and bleeding this is rarely the case. Be assured, C-sections are relatively safe in the West, but it should be stressed it is a major surgical procedure. Ultimately, an uncomplicated vaginal birth is far easier in the long term for the majority of women. Some women may feel an elective Caesarean is best for them, however, and any birth practitioner should respect that choice.

A breech baby is a common reason for elective Caesarean, as a breech (bum or feet first) birth carries greater risks. However, sections don't actually reduce the risks very much. In theory, giving birth to a breech baby naturally is often not as difficult as it is popularly portrayed to be. A skilled midwife or doctor will know how to encourage and aid the natural delivery of a breech baby. Unfortunately as birth in the mainstream becomes more medicalised midwives and obstetricians are no longer being taught these skills, so you may find that if you insist on a vaginal delivery what you get offered is assisted delivery involving epidural, a large episiotomy and forceps. These all carry significant risks, not the least of which is birth trauma. If you have your heart set on a natural delivery for your breech baby, request or hire a midwife who is skilled and experienced in this. It's also worth remembering that although as many as 15% of babies may present as breech at 32 weeks, by 38 weeks this goes down to less than 4%. Most babies will turn. You can encourage babies to turn with movement and massage with a specialist workshop such as Spinning Babies, founded by US midwife Gail Tully. With twins, it's common for the second baby to be breech right up until labour, but then turn in time to be born. If both twins are breech, you will usually be offered a C-section.

One of the main reasons emergency Caesarean rates have increased is that often the emergency has arisen because of unnecessary intervention in the first place; epidurals and inductions increase the risk of ending up in surgery, just as they increase the risk of episiotomies and forceps deliveries. Some women – and this would have been my choice also – would ultimately prefer a C-section to an assisted delivery, however, so as ever this is down to individual feeling. Remember, having an element of choice and control reduces birth trauma regardless of the type of birth you have.

A feeling of powerlessness and the longer recovery time may be key as to why rates of Postnatal Depression are higher in women who have had Caesareans. This is often down to the effects of birth trauma, which will be explored more in the next section. Studies by the *Journal of Child Psychology and Psychiatry* have also found that women who have had Caesareans are more likely to feel they are not bonding with their baby. As we saw in the last chapter, natural childbirth releases hormones important for both mother and baby, that promote bonding and responsiveness to one another.

So, how can you make your experience more positive if

you have your baby by C-section? Firstly, please don't feel, as is commonly reported by women, that you have somehow 'failed'. You and only you carried and birthed your baby, you just did it in a different way. As C-sections can be so challenging, I personally believe women who have them are exceptionally brave and strong and should be recognised as such.

As with an induction, if you are offered an elective section, do your research, use BRAINS and talk to someone about your hopes, fears and disappointments. Even if you are planning a natural birth, you may want to write a few 'just in case' pointers on your birth plan. You will then feel more in control if you have an unexpected section.

Hypnobirthing and other oxytocin boosting techniques are highly recommended as they will give you a hormone rush similar to natural childbirth and therefore promote calmness and bonding. You will find the birth visualisation adapted for C-sections at the end of this section.

Recently there has been a movement towards the 'Gentle Caesarean' aimed at making sections more natural for mother and baby. As research shows these modifications are resulting in shorter recovery times, decreased PND and increased feelings of well-being and bonding, medical caregivers are becoming more and more open to this. A 'gentle' C-section usually involves asking for the environment to be calmer and less clinical, so take your portable oxytocin kit with you, and more participation in the birth. This can be achieved by requesting an epidural or spinal block rather than a general anaesthetic so that you are awake, and if you're not squeamish you can watch the baby emerging from your womb through a clear drape. Alternatively, you can ask for the drape to be lowered as baby comes out. Ask for the baby to be placed immediately on your chest so you still have that all-important bonding period immediately after birth (or handed to your birth partner if this isn't feasible for any reason). You can then cuddle and even breastfeed your baby while you are being sutured. To make things more natural for baby, you can request delayed cord clamping and vaginal swabbing (more of these later).

If you have an emergency section, you are likely to still be contracting. A beautiful way of making a Caesarean more natural in this case is to request the baby is brought out on a contraction; in this way the womb still actively births the baby and it can even look as if the baby is making their own way out. A beautiful video showing a baby virtually 'walking out of the womb' recently went viral, and illustrated the amazing power and magic of birth, regardless of how it is achieved.

Exercise – Adapted Birth Visualisation for Caesarean

Just get yourself comfortable now... and now let your eyes find something on that wall... some spot or corner or a small object... and let your eyes rest on that point while you listen to the sound of my voice... hold your eyes open... and just look at that spot or that point... for a few moments... keep focusing on that spot... and your eyelids become heavy... heavier and heavier... blinking more and more... you can feel those eyelids becoming so heavy... but you just keep them open now... they may begin to water... that's okay... just keep them open... keep focusing... heavier and heavier... even though you want to close them you can keep them open for a few moments longer... and now close your eyes down... and as you close your eyes down you feel a wave of relaxation sweep through your entire body...

Now just focus on your breathing... breathing deeply... as you become so very deeply relaxed... breathing in... and breathing out... feeling your lungs and stomach expand as you breathe in... and your body relax so very deeply as you breathe out... relaxing more and more...

And now become aware of the quality of that relaxation... and imagine that relaxation spreading through the whole of your body... sweeping down from the top of your head to the tips of your toes... like a wave of relaxation... letting go... let go and relax every muscle in your body... that's right... really feel that relaxation from the crown of your head to the tips of your toes... feel how very good it feels to be this deeply relaxed...

And as deep as you are now... you can go ten times deeper. In a moment I am going to ask you to open your eyes... and then when you close them again you will go ten times deeper... so very deeply relaxed... relaxed in body and mind...

When you are ready I want you to imagine... in as much detail as is right for you now... a beautiful spiral staircase that takes you down to a special place... a safe place that is just for you... maybe the staircase has an ornate textured handrail, or maybe it is more plain and smooth, whatever is right for you now... either way it feels inviting to you and you go down... a step at a time... as I count from ten to one... and as I do so you can imagine yourself going down... a step at a time... going deeper and deeper... ten... nine... eight... see yourself going down... seven... six... hear your footsteps on the stairs, feel the stairs beneath your feet, and imagine yourself going deeper still... five... four... three... two... one... you step down and you can find yourself in your special place... and you can explore and take in all of the wonderful things there are to experience... all of the sights and sounds and smells... see what there is to see... feel what there is to feel... and just for a few moments take in all of the details of your special place... knowing that this safe place is just for you and you can return here whenever you choose...

Bring your attention now to your baby... knowing that as you are so very deeply relaxed so is your baby... And just as you are in your safe space so is your baby... deeply relaxed and calm inside you... safe and protected... and I would like you to imagine now that you are building a bubble around you both... a bubble that will keep you safe from worry... safe from fear... safe from stress... build this bubble around you... and see its colour... it can be any *colour you choose... as bright or as soft as you like... and stretch out your arms and feel the texture of this bubble all around you... it can be any texture you like... any tone... soft and smooth... or some other texture... this is your bubble and you can choose to create it however you wish now... and take a few minutes to feel and see this bubble around you... knowing that it keeps you and your baby safe and protected and able to deal with anything... and worries just bounce off this bubble and away... they just bounce off and away... shielding you from worry and stress... and you know that you are safe inside this bubble and that you can choose to recreate this bubble in your waking life any time you choose... any time you are going into a situation you may find stressful you can imagine this bubble around you... keeping you safe... it is yours to use any time you wish... send love to your baby... feel this love wrapping around your baby just like the bubble... safe and calm...*

Now imagine yourself at the birth... see yourself there with loving and supportive birth partners... excited about the arrival of your baby... greeting your baby with love and calm... see yourself relaxed and calm in your birthing environment... create around you and your baby all the things you need to feel calm and relaxed... safe and protected... know that everything will happen in just the right time... in just the right way... you have trust in your caregivers... you know they are going to assist you in birthing your baby... and you are excited and positive about birthing your baby in this way... knowing it is right and safe for you and your baby... and you send so much love to your baby... your body and your baby and your caregivers know exactly what to do... and you are calm and relaxed... safe and protected... feeling your body soften and relax... your womb soften and open... allowing your baby to move out of your womb and into your arms... calm and relaxed... safe and protected... see everything going smoothly and calmly... your body will heal swiftly and easily... you access your powerful subconscious healing powers... and you can just relax and let it happen... excited to meet your baby... welcoming your baby with love... surrounded with love and support... birthing your baby from your belly... such a miracle... welcoming your baby with love... calm and relaxed... imagine now you have your baby in your arms... greeting your baby... feel how very good that feels... feel that love and joy for your baby sweeping through your entire body... and take a few moments to just stay with that feeling... calm and relaxed... safe and protected... welcoming your baby with love...

And you can bring yourself back to your safe place now, ready to return to your waking life, knowing that you can bring these new feelings and new responses with you... and when you return you will return refreshed and alert.

Take a few more moments to enjoy your special place before you begin to wake up... feeling calm and refreshed... and you will begin to wake up as I count from one to five... fully refreshed... calm and alert... one... beginning to come up... two... becoming aware of the room around you... three... eyelids beginning to flicker... four... nearly there now... and five... OPEN YOUR EYES AND LOOK AROUND YOU, ALERT AND REFRESHED.

If you have previously had a Caesarean, you may feel it is now impossible to have a vaginal delivery. Subsequent sections are routinely offered as there is an increased risk of bleeding with a vaginal birth after a Caesarean (known as a VBAC) and an increased likelihood of an emergency section. However, there are many positive stories of women having successful VBACs and risks can often be mediated with appropriate care, so discuss your options with your caregivers and an independent body such as AIMS.

Resources/References

http://www.aims.org.uk/Journal/Vol10No3/breechCSvsNormal.htm

http://spinningbabies.com/

http://www.magicmum.com/wow-baby-walks-out-of-the-womb-during-gentle-cesarean/
https://www.mamanatural.com/gentle-cesarean/
http://vbacfacts.com/

Birth Trauma

The term 'birth trauma' is used here to refer to the after-effects on the mother of a physically, mentally or emotionally traumatic birth experience. Birth trauma commonly occurs after a birth that required emergency intervention, physical injury, heavy or unnecessary intervention, or any birth where the woman experienced high anxiety and particularly distressing feelings of powerlessness. A very quick birth that caused a state of shock can also result in trauma.

Birth trauma can result in anxiety, depression, feelings of numbness and even some resentment towards the baby, which in turn promotes intense guilt. PTSD is often diagnosed in more acute cases.

Symptoms of PTSD include:

- intense irritability
- panic attacks
- nightmares
- distressing flashbacks to the birth
- detached feelings towards loved ones (may include the baby)
- fear of impending disaster (often includes fear of something happening to the baby, which promotes acute distress)
- suicidal thoughts or feelings of despair

Do seek medical attention if you are suffering from any of the above.

You may even feel you may be suffering from birth trauma

but aren't sure. Perhaps there were positive and negative aspects to your birth, or your feelings have been invalidated by people saying 'at least the baby's healthy' or 'we all go through it' or variations of. These statements are meant well but can make the mother feel shut down or unheard, and she can begin to question her own experience. Or you may be unsure because some of the symptoms such as anxiety or sleep problems can be common with a new baby. If this is the case, ask yourself the following questions. If you find yourself with a significant amount of yes answers, you may well be experiencing or have experienced birth trauma.

Were there any times during the birth where you felt unsupported or uncared for?

At any time did you feel in danger of injury?

At any time did you feel your baby was in danger?

At any time did you feel significantly frightened, helpless, exposed, numb, severely detached, unable to go on or panicky?

If you answered 'yes' to any of the above, ask yourself: since the birth have you experienced difficulty sleeping, an exaggerated startle response, poor concentration, depression or anxiety?

Do you try and avoid remembering certain aspects of the birth?

If you have experienced a traumatic birth previously, you may be feeling increased anxiety around your impending birth. This is particularly acute if you have never had a chance to talk through the birth and your feelings about it with a compassionate and non-judgmental ear – known as 'debriefing'. Finding someone to do this with can be incredibly healing. There are online communities for women who have been through a traumatic birth experience which can be helpful for sharing stories. Do bear in mind though that if you are currently pregnant hearing traumatic stories may increase your anxiety.

Guilt and feelings of having done something wrong often accompany birth trauma. Although these feelings are typical, they aren't true. *It wasn't your fault.* And armed with your new knowledge, positive birthing techniques and ways to calm anxiety, this time around may bring profound healing.

You may notice during this book that I'm a big fan of healing rituals. Ritual has been proven to heal on a psychological, spiritual and physiological level, and can help us reshape the narratives we live by. A ritual often recommended for birth trauma is known as 'rebirthing' or 'birth reclaiming' where you are guided through a ritual or visualisation adapted to your needs to help you release the trauma and envision and experience the birth as you would have liked it to be. This can be done regardless of how old your child now is, as they don't necessarily need to be present. Seek out a ritual therapist who offers birth reclaiming and if possible have your original birth partners there too. This can be a deeply healing experience.

While you're pregnant, intense therapy that asks you to repeatedly relive the trauma is not advised. This can be highly distressing, which floods your body with stress hormones and in turn upsets baby, so please bear that in mind when seeking therapy for birth trauma. A favourite technique of mine, which allows for processing of traumatic events without the need for intense reliving of the experience, is Emotional Freedom Technique or EFT. Popularly known as 'tapping', EFT is a fast, simple and effective therapy that has astounded researchers and psychotherapists with its ability to swiftly resolve both emotional and physical issues. Blending the best of Eastern alternative therapies with Western psychotherapy, EFT works by applying finger pressure to points along the body's meridian lines, using the same energy field as acupuncture, while simultaneously using affirmation and focused talking therapy.

EFT has been proven to help people overcome trauma, phobias, emotional issues and even chronic pain swiftly and effectively. It can also be used with positive affirmation and visualisation to boost self-confidence and self-esteem. It is also easily taught and can be self-administered, making it an empowering form of therapy.

Although I recommend you seek out a face-to-face therapist to truly process birth trauma, you can use the introduction to EFT for Birth Trauma below (or download it from the accompanying website) to see if this is something you feel may be helpful for you, or as a quick anxiety-relieving boost.

Introduction to EFT – Birth Trauma

Rate your current feelings of anxiety on a scale of one to ten.

With one hand, lightly 'Karate chop' in a repetitive tapping motion the outside of the other hand midway between the wrist and base of the fingers. As you do so say aloud to yourself three times, 'Even though my last birth has left me anxious and afraid, I deeply and completely accept myself.' If you struggle with that phrase, make it less intense, for example, 'Even though my last birth didn't go how I wanted it to, I am willing to accept my experience now.'

Using the fingertips of your index and middle fingers of your tapping hand, lightly tap repeatedly on the following points while saying aloud the accompanying phrases:

Above the eyebrow: 'I release the pain from my last birth.'
Outside corner of the eye: 'I release the suffering.'
Under the eye: 'I release the disappointment.'
Under the nose: 'I release the fear.'
Middle of chin: 'I release the blame of self and others.'
Collarbone: 'I release the anger.'
Underneath the armpit, halfway down the ribs: 'I release the physical tension.'
Crown of the head: 'I accept and honour my experience of birth and

release the feelings I have been holding.'

Now rate your current anxiety on a scale of one to ten. If it hasn't lowered to at least a two, repeat this two more times. You may like to repeat it anyway.

If you feel a little tearful during this, it's OK. Carry on and let the feelings rise and fall.

If you are currently pregnant, move on to the next round of tapping. Do this three times:

Side of hand: 'Even though I am anxious (or insert your own appropriate word) about this birth, I deeply and completely accept myself.'
Above eyebrow: 'This birth will be different.'
Side of eye: 'This birth will be full of joy.'
Under the eye: 'I will feel in control.'
Under the nose: 'I will be empowered to make good choices.'
Middle of chin: 'I will feel supported and loved.'
Collarbone: 'I look forward to this birth.'
Under arm: 'I am preparing for a positive birth.'
Crown of head: 'I reclaim all of my births as powerful transformative experiences. I reclaim my birthing power. I am mother. I am powerful.' (If you feel so inclined, shout or roar this last phrase!)

You can use this whole exercise, or either round of tapping, whenever and as often as you like.

Resources/References
Birth Crisis – Sheila Kitzinger (Routledge, 2006)
https://www.bellybelly.com.au/birth/birth-reclaiming-ceremony/
http://www.solaceformothers.org/
http://www.unfoldyourwings.co.uk/

Birth for Sexual Abuse Survivors

An often overlooked factor in women's anxiety and fear around birth is a history of sexual abuse and assault. Particularly with a highly medicalised birth which often involves a glut of vaginal exams, often by a male caregiver, feelings of disempowerment and physical trauma to the genitals such as an episiotomy, the parallels are obvious. And for women who are survivors of sexual violence, certain aspects of birth can be triggering and traumatic. Sadly, this is too often an overlooked area. Considering the high levels of sexual assault on women, much more awareness of this issue is needed.

Fear of birth can be acute for abuse survivors, with common issues including a fear of being helpless, being exposed, distrust of caregivers particularly males, finding any intervention – especially vaginal exams – triggering, and even a sense of distrust or dislike towards the baby as on some level the baby is seen as a perpetrator. This last can cause particular distress as the mother is in conflict with her natural love for the baby against her trauma-induced fear, and often feels intense guilt and worry that she won't bond with her child. Coupled with the fact that not many people are talking about this, and staff on maternity wards have rarely had training in this area, and this can seem like an insurmountable obstacle. If this is you or anyone you know, please be assured that with a little understanding and awareness, plus the use and practice of the techniques described in the previous chapters, sexual abuse survivors can often find that childbirth becomes, rather than a traumatic event, a profoundly healing one. Just as the body is a key factor in the trauma, it is a key factor in healing. An empowering and powerful birth experience, according to energy medicine experts, can transform a woman's relationship to her body and her sexuality. Pregnancy yoga, with trauma-focused care, can also provide somatic healing and help to promote positive feelings approaching birth. Hypnobirthing in particular both relieves anxiety and promotes bonding. The guided visualisation in Chapter Five for late pregnancy also helps foster connection between mother and baby.

An undisturbed, unmedicalised birth is recommended in this case, and if this isn't possible, have a look over your options and think about how you might be able to reduce the factors that you personally find upsetting or triggering. Talk to your caregivers. You don't need to give them any more information other than: 'For mental health reasons/because of previous experience, it is crucial that this does/does not happen/how can this be made easier for me?' Or if your birth partner is aware of your history, you can ask them to advocate for you. For example vaginal examinations may be a source of stress. In a routine birth with no complications, vaginal exams are largely unnecessary. They are primarily to check dilation, yet are often far from accurate, and can put women under pressure by feeling like they should be dilating at a certain rate. Birth doesn't happen on a clock. So you can ask that internal exams be kept to an absolute minimum or not performed at all unless there is an absolute emergency. If you do choose to have them, make your caregiver aware that you find them distressing and ask for gentleness and consideration. Most caregivers will go out of their way to make the experience as pleasant as possible. If their response is less than compassionate, ask for another caregiver. You can use mindfulness or hypnobirthing during the exam or ask for gas and air (be aware this can make you very 'spacey').

Supportive birth companions are vital, so you may consider hiring a doula you feel comfortable confiding in if you don't feel you have enough support. She will be there to listen to your fears, allow you to share your story with compassion and cheer you on.

Of course, if you are suffering with severe PTSD or other mental health issues, do consult your doctor. A perinatal psychiatrist can give you an extra level of support and, depending on maternity resources in your area or country, you are likely to be offered ongoing support in the postnatal period. The techniques in the previous chapters can all be used as complementary to your medical care plan.

Therapy is a powerful healer for sexual abuse, but it is important to remember that during pregnancy it's better for you and baby to be as relaxed and calm as possible, so avoid therapies that are likely to upset you – an 'it gets worse before it gets better' approach – or ask you to relive the trauma. Very gentle inner child hypnosis may help, and holistic therapies, compassion-focused counselling or EFT will be gentler modalities to work with. There is an adapted version of the previous EFT script below if you would like to try this (and more scripts are available on the website accompanying this book) but bear in mind that as with all therapies face-to-face support is unparalleled. Healing rituals and birth art provide a spiritual element to healing, addressing the 'soul loss' (or in therapy speak disassociation) that often occurs after sexual abuse. You may also find women's circles, often known as Red Tents, helpful and deeply healing. This is a growing movement across the world, where women come together on a regular basis to share stories and healing.

EFT Script – Birth Anxiety for Sexual Abuse Survivors

Rate your current feelings of anxiety on a scale of one to ten.

With one hand, lightly 'Karate chop' in a repetitive tapping motion the outside of the other hand midway between the wrist and base of the fingers. As you do so say aloud to yourself three times, 'Even though my experience of sexual abuse/trauma has left me anxious and afraid, I deeply and completely accept myself.' If you struggle with that phrase, make it less intense, for example: 'Even though my experiences have affected my feelings towards the birth, I am willing to believe it will be OK.'

Using the fingertips of your index and middle fingers of your tapping hand, lightly tap repeatedly on the following points while saying aloud the accompanying phrases:

Above the eyebrow: 'I release the pain from my experience.'
Outside corner of the eye: 'I release the suffering.'
Under the eye: 'I release the disappointment.'
Under the nose: 'I release the fear.'
Middle of chin: 'I release the blame of self. It was not my fault. It was not my fault. It was not my fault.'
Collarbone: 'I release the anger.'
Underneath the armpit, halfway down the ribs: 'I release the physical trauma.'
Crown of the head: 'My experience was awful, but I am healing and moving forward.'
Go back to above the eyebrow: 'I release my anxiety around the birth.'
Side of the eye: 'The past does not determine my future.'
Outside corner of the eye: 'I find ways to manage this anxiety.'
Under the eye: 'I am willing to believe this birth can heal me.'
Under the nose: 'I release the fear.'
Middle of chin: 'I will be OK.'
Collarbone: 'I can do this.'
Underneath the armpit, halfway down the ribs: 'I heal my body and heart.'
Crown of the head: 'I am willing to accept this birth can heal me and I can have a positive experience.'

Now rate your current anxiety on a scale of one to ten. If it hasn't lowered to at least a two, repeat this two more times. You may like to repeat it anyway.

If you feel a little tearful during this, it's OK. Carry on and let the feelings rise and fall.

Move on to the next round of tapping. Do this three times:

Side of hand: 'Even though I am anxious (or insert your own appropriate word) about the birth of my baby, I deeply and completely accept myself.'
Above eyebrow: 'This birth is a healing event.'
Side of eye: 'This birth will be full of joy.'
Under the eye: 'I will feel in control.'
Under the nose: 'I will be empowered to make good choices.'
Middle of chin: 'I will feel supported and loved.'
Collarbone: 'I look forward to this birth.'
Under arm: 'I am preparing for a positive birth.'
Crown of head: 'I reclaim my body. I reclaim my birthing power. I am mother. I am powerful.' (If you feel so inclined, shout or roar this last phrase!)

You can use this whole exercise, or either round of tapping, whenever and as often as you like.

Resources/References

http://birthwithoutfearblog.com/2012/09/12/sexual-abuse-and-birth2/
http://www.pandys.org/articles/childbirthafterrape.pdf
http://www.thebreathenetwork.org/transcending-the-trauma-of-sexual-violence-with-yoga
When Survivors Give Birth – Penny Simkin (Classic Day, 2004)

Previous Pregnancy Loss

Sadly, many women suffer the pain of abortion, miscarriage and even stillbirth. Having had these experiences prior to your current pregnancy can provoke grief, anxiety and even guilt. This varies, woman to woman, just as the scenarios of pregnancy loss vary. A woman who had a miscarriage some years ago may feel very different to a woman who has recently had a succession of losses while desperately trying for a baby. Just as a woman who had a past abortion which was entirely her own choice is likely to feel differently about this during her new pregnancy, than a woman who still grieves the abortion she feels she had no choice but to go through with. Anyone who has suffered a stillbirth may feel intense anxiety and is likely to still be going through the grief process.

Although everyone grieves differently, the grief and loss cycle has been noted to have distinct rhythms common to most experiences. There is no time frame to this and many women may find they cycle through the process repeatedly, follow a different order, or skip one of the stages completely. I describe it here as a guide only. How you currently feel about your previous pregnancy loss will be affected by where you are in this cycle. Generally, the grief and loss cycle is described in five stages:

- Denial. Initially following a loss, we often go into a state of shock where we cannot, or will not allow ourselves to, accept what has happened. This can be characterised by a state of numbness, where the intensity of feelings has yet to emerge. Although this stage is often short, it is possible to become stuck, to disassociate or repress the emotions and event, only for them to resurface years later. This may be the case for women who have been through a miscarriage or abortion and felt they were expected to 'get on with it' and were never able to process their experience.

- Anger. Intense feelings will arise here with anger often a big factor, whether at ourselves, loved ones, someone we hold responsible, or even God. We feel we need someone to blame in order to make sense of what has happened. There is a sort of safety in anger; it often feels easier to navigate than the overwhelming feelings of loss that lie behind it. To get stuck in it, however, can lead to bitterness, depression and a sense of disconnection from others and life, as well as feelings of rejection and abandonment.

- Bargaining. This is where we begin to ruminate on 'what ifs' and often also project these into the future. 'Just let me get pregnant and I'll be a better wife', for example, or 'I'll go to church every Sunday; just let this relationship work'. These first three stages may often be cycled through repeatedly and quite rapidly before moving on.

- Depression. The loss has been acknowledged, but it feels as if the grieving will go on forever. Lethargy, sadness or numbness may set in and this phase can feel never-ending. In fact, it is the darkness before the dawn, though there is a danger of becoming 'stuck' in it, particularly where there have been repeated situations of loss in someone's life.

- Acceptance. Some form of equilibrium has been reached. Although there will always be sadness about the situation, it is no longer debilitating or overwhelming. Life has resumed to 'normal' or in some cases changed completely, but that change has been settled into. In the case of pregnancy loss, however, some women may find that they thought they were in acceptance, only to find their new pregnancy causes old feelings to resurface.

It's important to remember that however you feel about your past experiences and how this affects you now, your feelings are valid, and deserve to be honoured. If you feel, as so many women who have suffered pregnancy loss do, that you were never able to grieve fully, then find someone you can talk through the story of your experience with. A compassion-focused therapist or an empathetic, non-judgmental friend may be ideal. Ritual again can also be a powerful way to integrate and begin to release our losses. You will find some ideas in the Resources below. There are also many healing therapists who can conduct this for you; indeed I would urge you to do this with your partner, friend, family member or doula if you don't have a therapist.

Exercise – Altar for the Lost Ones

Often women – and their male partners too – who experience pregnancy loss feel their experience is dismissed as something to 'get over'. Even in the case of a stillbirth, others often fail to appreciate the intensity of the grief that can ensue. A way of marking the experience, of acknowledging the life that existed, albeit for a short time, can be to create an altar that honours that life and the loss of it.

An altar is a focal point in your home and can be as simple as a candle and a piece of ribbon on a bedside table or an entire cabinet devoted to its purpose filled with objects and talismans that are meaningful to you. Ideas for things to include on an altar for this purpose include:

- *any keepsakes of your baby ie scans, a piece of fabric from a blanket, a positive pregnancy test etc*
- *artwork or writing you have produced about your experience*
- *candles*
- *statues – perhaps of a grieving woman or mother and child or angels*
- *flowers*
- *anything that feels personally relevant to you*

Resources/References

https://www.babycenter.com/0_staying-positive-when-youre-pregnant-again-after-a-loss_9181.bc
https://ritualwell.org/pregnancy-loss
https://www.sands.org.uk/
http://pregnancyloss.info/2009/11/dia-de-los-muertos/
http://www.brigidsgrove.com/miscarriage-memorial/

Part Two – Happy Birth, Happy Baby

There are words in the soul of a newborn baby,
waiting and wanting to be written.
Toba Beta

Chapter Four – How Birth Affects Your Baby's Health

Birth is a normal function of biology, employing the combined physiology of mother and baby working together to bring baby to mother's arms.
Carla Hartley

The next two chapters focus primarily on your baby's experience of birth and how it may affect them in both the short and long term. Only for ease of reference and reading have I separated them into two, focusing first on the physiological aspects and then the psychological. The truth of course is that both mind and body affect each other and relate to each other as parts of a symbiotic whole. Much the same as a woman and her unborn baby are two parts of a whole (and this does not just end at birth, as any mother knows).

Before we go on, I would like to reassure women reading this who have had previous children: no, you haven't screwed them up for life because you didn't have a natural birth or breastfeed. Feeling guilty and worrying we could have done more seems to go hand in hand with motherhood, particularly in a society that both devalues us and then seeks to blame us for many of society's ills. I refuse to contribute to this. Nevertheless, my first reaction when I began to learn about woman-centred birth and the effects upon baby's health was to mentally beat myself up for not breastfeeding my first son or having immediate contact. Although I was never offered the latter, I still blamed myself. When he then went on to develop childhood asthma I was convinced it was down to my failings. The truth is I will never know whether, had I breastfed, he would still have gone on to develop asthma or not; all I can say is that it may have been a contributing factor. Birth is important, yet still only one factor in a child's life. My son 'grew out' of his asthma and is now one of the healthiest teenagers I know. Don't blame yourself for not knowing things you didn't know, that your medical caregivers also didn't know or weren't telling you. Now is the time that matters.

If you find yourself having intense feelings of guilt about something that happened during a previous birth, I would suggest you read the section on birth trauma as this is often one of the symptoms. Give yourself the space to heal and then move forward to embrace your new experience. Something that personally helped me with those feelings was to ask my own mother about my birth and what she knew about hers. Not in the sense of swapping horrific stories, but an exploration into what she thought and felt and wished for. I discovered things I had never known about my mother and grandmother, and it also became clear to me just how important it is that as women we stop feeling guilty for absolutely everything and instead reclaim our innate strength and compassion. If you're unable to have this conversation with your mother or other older female figure, consider joining a Red Tent. These are gatherings of women from all communities where women share and heal their stories, including around birth and motherhood.

So, how to make birth healthy and positive for baby as much as for ourselves? Firstly, everything we covered in Part One will be as good for your baby as it is for you. When you're relaxed, baby is relaxed. When you're being flooded with oxytocin, so is baby. I put the section for mamas first not just because it's about time they were put first, but also because to care for the mother *is* to care for the child.

We will look more at psychological aspects of birth such as bonding and your baby's emotional development in the next chapter. Firstly, let's have a look at recent research into how certain aspects of the birth process can impact your baby's future health.

Primal Health

Although very recent research into the microbiome and epigenetics show just how important to future health a woman-centred, more natural birth is, on a global as well as individual scale, these ideas are not new. Before the powers-that-be in the medical childbirth world began to realise that Mother Nature and, indeed, mothers themselves had it right all along, Michel Odent was campaigning for greater awareness in this area. Back in 1986 he published *Primal Health* arguing that the birth and infancy period was critical for our future well-being.

Odent focused this research on the 'primal adaptive system' or the complex network of physical systems such as the nervous and immune, along with our hormones and other factors, that make up our basic health. This adaptive system reaches maturity during the primal period from in the womb to our first birthday, with birth playing a large role. According to Odent, this forms our health 'blueprint' and we will spend the rest of our lives either optimising this or seeking to make up for what we have missed. So achieving good primal health gives us a head start for well-being in later life. Although this may have been a groundbreaking concept to Western science, Eastern medicine traditions had been saying for a long time that the foetal period, birth and infancy formed the foundation for the rest of our life.

Primal health research began to find correlations between problems at birth, especially the separation of mother and baby, and rates of what researchers call the 'diseases of Western civilisation'. These include depression, cancer, autoimmune disorders and even alcoholism and schizophrenia.

Awareness of the psychological effects of a difficult birth gradually became more widespread, but only recently did the realisation that how we are born affects us on a physiological level become mainstream. Now, with the discovery of the microbiome, we are starting to understand just how and why this is. As we will see, Nature is incredibly clever.

The Microbiome

You are full of bacteria. And not just in the obvious places, or on your hands from touching external objects. Bacteria lives in our cells, has merged with them and aided our evolution. Although it varies from person to person, the percentage of bacteria to human cells in our bodies may be as much as ninety to ten. We have around one trillion microbes living in us. If this makes you feel slightly queasy, I believe this is really quite amazing. Each one of us is more than an individual human; each one of us is a complete ecosystem. Each one of us has a wholly unique microbiome, much like a fingerprint.

Usually, we live in complete harmony with our microbiome but when things become out of balance, we get ill. The microbiome in our gut has been heavily studied and it has been discovered how the typical Western diet and the overuse of antibiotics damages this harmony and can result in a variety of diseases, from stubborn viruses to life-threatening ailments.

What does this have to do with birth? Quite a lot.

When a baby is born the main seeding of its own microbiome occurs. This, just like Michel Odent's 'primal adaptive system', lays a foundation for future health.

Although in some mothers there may be bacteria present in the placenta, the womb is a largely sterile environment. Yet in late pregnancy, the mother's microbiome changes. Especially in the vagina the bacteria lactobacilli (the 'good' bacteria we get in yoghurts) increases drastically. As the baby moves down the birth canal it becomes coated in this healthy bacteria, soaks it up like a little sponge, and so its own microbiome is seeded. This also has positive effects for the baby's immune system and metabolism. This all happens with nature's perfect timing. Intervention – particularly elective Caesarean in which the baby is not exposed to the mother's vagina at all – can greatly interfere with this crucial event. Lactobacilli also has the immediate positive effect of helping to break down lactose in breast milk.

The microbiome continues to be seeded in the pivotal time after birth and this is one of the reasons immediate skin-to-skin contact between mother and baby is so important, as the infant continues to absorb the mother's bacteria through the skin. Breastfeeding, particularly a first feed after birth, is also highly important for establishing friendly gut bacteria in your baby's body.

Thankfully much of the Western world is catching on to how important skin-to-skin contact is and it is usually encouraged whole-heartedly in hospitals, but this does depend on where you live, so this will probably be something you want to write in big letters on your birth plan. I find it tragic that only now are medical staff beginning to advise mothers to hold their babies in close contact immediately after birth, something mothers and babies have instinctively done since the dawn of time. This has resulted in generations of mums and newborns being separated at a time when nature has designed them to be together. It wouldn't be entirely fair to blame medical staff for this though; separation of mother and baby, particularly among the 'upper classes', has been prevalent since medieval times.

What if you have a C-section? You can ask for vaginal swabbing to be done. This is where a sterile swab is used to collect some of the vaginal fluid before delivery, then immediately after birth this is wiped around the baby's mouth. Studies have shown this goes a long way towards restoring the seeding process. You can also still request immediate skin-to-skin contact and breastfeed your baby soon after birth. I believe breastfeeding to be an individual decision, but even if you are planning to formula feed you might want to give your baby an initial breastfeed to help with this microbiome and immune system boosting, especially if you have had a Caesarean.

Natural Second Stage

Stages are something of a misnomer when it comes to birth as no woman labours on a clock, yet the time when your cervix has fully dilated and the baby moves down the birth canal and emerges into the outside world is known as 'second stage'. In a medicalised birth this may involve a woman on her back, possibly restrained by monitors, catheters or IV lines, with overzealous midwives telling her to 'Push!' and 'Pant!' with her chin tucked into her chest. This usually leaves the mother tense, stressed and exhausted, all of which is counterproductive to the natural birth process. Your body already wants and knows how to birth your baby, there is no need to force it if things have been going well so far. An exception to this may be if you have had a spinal block as you are numb to sensations and therefore your body's feedback cues; another way epidural interferes with a natural process. Opiates too may leave you feeling disconnected from bodily sensation. This is one of the reasons a medicalised second stage is more likely to lead to further medicalisation: either an episiotomy and forceps or ventouse extraction or an emergency C-section.

All being well, this can be avoided by bringing your breathing and relaxation techniques to second stage and letting your body do what it needs to do. Any hypnobirthing class will teach you how to 'breathe the baby down' and stay relaxed, which assists rather than hinders the natural expulsion process. As long as your baby is in no distress, there is no reason why this stage has to be a race. In fact, over management of this stage results in a stressed mother and a stressed baby, which can then result in harmful interventions.

There are a few variations on breathing techniques to help your baby move down; the following is my personal favourite:

Exercise – Vagina Breathing

I have considered calling this something different and more 'flowery', as a similar technique is called 'J Breath' because of the shape it makes. However, the phrase was coined by a client in a hypnobirthing class and it seems to have stuck, so here's how your vagina can literally exhale your baby...

Take a deep breath in, consciously relaxing your face, jaw and shoulders. You may like to do a mindfulness or relaxation technique (see Chapter Seven) first to relax yourself further.

As you breathe out, feel the breath moving down your body to your baby and then out through your vagina, consciously placing your attention at the opening. It may take a few attempts, but you will feel the tissues in your vagina warming and expanding as you do this, and you can sense how this would be helpful in easing your baby down and out.

Keep practising, particularly in the run-up to the birth. As you breathe out through your vagina try visualising it relaxing and opening. Another common hypnobirthing technique is to visualise a flower opening.

Using mindfulness and breathing techniques during second stage will relax you and be less stressful for your baby, but don't think that means you have to be quiet and still during it. As baby moves down and the pressure gets more intense, some women find that the exhale of the Vagina Breath turns into a hum, a growl, a roar or even singing! Go with what you feel. One woman reported that the breath itself began to feel like fiery energy moving through her, like 'liquid gold'. You may also like to use this as a visualisation.

Speaking of fiery energy, the moments when the baby's head begins to emerge, when your vaginal tissues are stretched to the fullest, is known as crowning or informally as 'the ring of fire'. It's intense, but thankfully over quickly, and the final hurdle before your beautiful baby emerges into your arms. Many women worry about tearing at this stage; so much so that in some countries women will routinely ask for an episiotomy. We discussed this in Chapter Three, so I will just reiterate here that a natural tear is nearly always preferable and less traumatic. There are a few exceptions of course, but generally women report healing much faster than after an episiotomy, and episiotomies are more likely to result in long-term damage. Using the techniques described will greatly decrease your risk of tearing, as will the massage technique in Chapter Three. Using the massage regularly is also a good way to experience what crowning may feel like.

This is all very important for your baby as well as you as a natural second stage is less likely to lead to foetal distress, as well as physical trauma from forceps or a ventouse. In the US, nearly 3% of babies are born with physical injury from an assisted delivery. I'm sure we would all prefer, given the choice, to be 'breathed out' of our mother's womb than dragged from it with metal tools. In rare cases assisted delivery may be necessary, and you can help the process along by using the breathing techniques. A good caregiver will be as gentle as possible; don't be afraid to ask for this.

The end of second stage is the birth of your baby. As we have seen, immediate skin-to-skin contact is optimal for both health and well-being and will also soothe your baby. Your baby is likely to be covered in vernix, a waxy substance that has been protecting their delicate skin. Hospital routine is to wash this off; you can ask for baby to be washed while on your chest. However, it is better for baby if washing is postponed until you take your baby home, as vernix is shown to protect your baby from infection and also protect its skin from the strange elements of a new world.

Skin to Skin for Premature Babies

Traditionally premature babies were kept in constant contact with the mother, which kept them warm, encouraged them to thrive and helped establish breastfeeding. Now a premature baby in modern society is more likely to be separated from the mother and placed in an incubator. While there is no doubt that this can save lives, meaning that babies now have much greater chances of survival much earlier on, the lack of skin contact can be detrimental for the baby and heartbreaking for the mother. According to Professor Joy Lawn from the London School of Hygiene, lots of skin contact, known as 'kangaroo care', is more effective than intensive care for babies born between 32–38 weeks. Before 32 weeks babies need help to breathe, but after this time their primary needs are helped with feeding and regulating their temperature. They're also more prone to infection. Lawn believes after extensive research that these needs are better met through breastfeeding and near constant contact with the mother than they are in an incubator. In parts of Africa, where neonatal units are not available, kangaroo care is saving lives. If your baby is born after 32 weeks you might want to discuss this with your caregivers and hospital and see what your options are. While you may not be able to take your baby home, you can request facilities to stay at the hospital in close contact with your newborn. This is also crucial for establishing breastfeeding.

If your baby is born with immature lungs or breathing capacities and has to be incubated, there are ways you can simulate a more natural process. Fabric squares are often used – you keep these close to your skin and then they are placed next to baby, you can pump your breast milk for them, and most incubators now will allow for some touch, as hospitals recognise the importance of this. In some units such as the Small Baby Unit in California, at the Children's Hospital of Orange County, lights are kept dimmed and sounds used to simulate the environment of the womb as much as possible. If you have a very premature baby, make it clear to your caregivers you want as much contact with your baby as is safe, and ask them what they are doing to make the neonatal units as natural for babies as possible.

Delayed Cord Clamping

In the traditional medical model, cords were cut within the first moments of the baby emerging into the world, before it had stopped pulsing. Now the World Health Organization states that cords should never be cut within the first minute, and ideally the cord should not be cut or clamped until all the blood has stopped flowing from the placenta to the baby, usually after 3 minutes.

Your baby needs that blood. The placenta's final function is to transfer this through the cord to your baby, and this makes up to a third of your baby's total blood. Cutting the cord too quickly means most of this will never reach the infant and this puts them at greater risk of iron deficiency which in turn can affect neurological development. This lack of needed blood also affects baby's weight. Cutting the cord too early may also bear risks to the mother by increasing the possibility of haemorrhage.

Most caregivers are now becoming aware of this, but as ever progress can be both patchy and slow. Erasmus Darwin spoke about the importance of delayed cord clamping back in 1800! You can ask if it is routine and if not put it on your birth plan. For a great demonstration of what happens when the cord is cut early, watch the video by birth expert Penny Simkin that is listed in the resources.

Natural Third Stage

The 'third stage' of labour is the time between the baby being born and the removal of the placenta. This then is that all-important time for both bonding and the laying of foundations for future health. It is typical in many places for this stage to be what is called 'actively managed' rather than 'physiologically managed' even when the rest of the birth has been very natural and woman-centred.

An actively managed third stage involves giving the mother an injection in her thigh of prophylactic uterotonic, which causes the placenta to detach quickly from the womb wall, and often cord traction, where the cord is pulled and massaged to encourage the release of the placenta. A physiologically managed third stage is where the placenta is left to emerge by itself; the womb will contract and the placenta will, usually quite easily, be delivered along with the membranes.

Active management has been shown to have a slightly

smaller chance of heavy bleeding and anaemia after birth, where both cord traction and the drug are used. Cord traction or rough massaging of the abdomen in an otherwise physiological stage can result in increased bleeding and pain for the mother. Some women may consider the risks to outweigh the benefits, however, as active management shows increases in blood pressure, pain after birth, nausea and increased vaginal bleeding in the postnatal stage.

If you have decided on a natural – or as natural as possible depending on your circumstances – birth, then it would make sense to continue this with the third stage, particularly as it means less interruption during that all-important first hour after birth where you are cuddling and probably feeding your newborn. Other women may want to get the placenta delivered as quickly as possible, so they can then carry on with that blissful time without midwives popping in to see if you have delivered the placenta yet!

The UK Royal College of Midwives states that women should be fully supported in a decision to have an uninterrupted, physiologically managed third stage, but that active management would be recommended if the placenta isn't delivered within an hour.

Lotus Birth

Talking about cords and placenta delivery leads me on to a recent trend among natural childbirth advocates: that of the 'lotus birth'. This is where the cord is not cut, both it and the placenta are left attached to the baby. It usually falls off at around three to four days, although this may be extended to around ten days in more humid climates.

Some lotus birth advocates claim that this helps prevent infection and optimises the positive effects of delayed cord clamping, yet there is little evidence to show health benefits of leaving the placenta attached. It often, however, has deep significance on an emotional and spiritual level for the parents, who believe the 'holy trinity' of baby, cord and placenta should be kept intact until nature decides otherwise. There may be psychological benefits for the baby in allowing the placenta to stay attached; after all a baby in the womb has been sharing the space with the placenta its entire life, and keeping it attached may help ease the transition into the world. Babies who are lotus birthed are often seen holding on to the cord while they sleep.

The first response I often get from people when I ask them what they think about lotus births is often: 'But doesn't it smell?' Indeed, the placenta and cord will begin to rot quite quickly after birth. This is managed by seasoning and covering the placenta with herbs that are changed daily, wrapped in muslin and placed in a bag made especially for the purpose.

It really is the ultimate in undisturbed birth and if it resonates with you this may be something you wish to explore in more detail.

Vitamin K

It has been routine since 1944 to give infants a shot of Vitamin K soon after birth, and this has been crucial in preventing haemorrhage in newborns. However, the shot can contain more than 20,000 times the amount your baby actually needs, which can lead to increased rates of infection. It must also be incredibly traumatic for a little baby who has just emerged into an utterly strange environment to have a large syringe pushed painfully into their leg.

You do have the right to refuse the Vitamin K, but bear in mind most babies born in Western society will be deficient in this vitamin. A safer and less traumatic alternative is for Vitamin K oral drops to be given to baby, which provides a far safer dose. This is thankfully becoming routine, much like skin-to-skin contact and delayed cord clamping, but again it depends on where you live so you can make a point of requesting it.

Resources/References

http://primalhealthresearch.com/

http://microbirth.com/

https://www.mommypotamus.com/benefits-of-skin-to-skin/

http://www.medicalnewstoday.com/articles/305950.php

https://mybirthcompanion.com/penny-simkin-on-delayed-cord-clamping/

http://www.sacredbirthing.com/lotus-birth/

http://articles.mercola.com/sites/articles/archive/2010/03/27/high-risks-to-your-baby-from-vitamin-k-shot-they-dont-warn-you-about.aspx

Placenta: the Forgotten Chakra – Robin Lim (1st World Library, 2015)

Chapter Five – How Birth Affects Your Baby's Mind

A baby is born with a need to be loved and never outgrows it.
Frank A. Clark

Nature has designed for a mother and her newborn to fall in love with each other.

Watch videos of natural, undisturbed birth and you will see the baby emerging from its mother's womb and almost crawling up her body to the breast. The mother's smell and skin comfort the baby and let him or her know they are safe. Oxytocin levels are high as baby opens its eyes for the first time and turns its unfocused gaze upon the centre of its world. The intense attachment that forms is like nothing else on earth and this fundamental evolutionary truth was recognised long before modern psychology. Even the Bible declares God's love to be like that of a mother's!

This intense love may well feel heavenly yet also has a practical evolutionary purpose. Baby humans are helpless and utterly dependent for a long time. What else but an intense bond could make a woman devote her entire being to nurturing someone else, and find joy in doing so?

Bonding at Birth and Newborn Attachment

Recent modern practices then that separated mother and child at birth were against all common and natural sense. Nevertheless they were highly regarded at the time. Although thankfully now rapidly being replaced by knowledge of the importance of the immediate hour after birth and skin contact, this can still happen in some areas or situations. Rushed hospital staff trying to see to many different women at once often see this crucial bonding time as another phase to be ticked off before moving on to the next. An obligatory twenty minutes of skin contact may be given in some UK NHS hospitals before the room is full of medical staff again, weighing and measuring your baby. A recent report on maternity services in the UK cited women stating they felt like cattle on a conveyer belt when having a hospital birth. This may be one very good reason to choose a home birth or midwife-led birthing centre rather than a maternity ward. However, you and your baby do not have to conform to any time frame. You can request an uninterrupted first hour and that checks on baby be performed while he or she remains on your chest. This time is sacred and doesn't take place against a clock, so don't let anyone pressure you. These are the moments you may need a birth plan and/or a birth partner to advocate for you. Known as the 'Sacred Hour' or 'Holy Hour' in some cultures, birth activists are reclaiming this time in the Western medical world.

The psychological benefits of an undisturbed birth and bonding period are many and profound, and researchers and experts are learning and discovering more and more about this all the time. We are certainly a long way from the standard hospital practices of the early 1900s when women were given drugs during childbirth that rendered them virtually unconscious and incapable of interacting with their babies for some hours or even days, during which time babies would be given basic care in hospital nurseries. It was often believed at the time that this protected babies against infection by the mother! This is tragically ironic given what we now know about the microbiome.

Unless women had home births – more common among the working classes as there was little free health care available back then – this remained a standard model of birth until into the fifties and sixties, when it was finally understood that general anaesthetic was physically harmful to newborns. As further research into the positive health benefits of skin to skin and breastfeeding after birth was conducted the medical model began finally, slowly to change.

These changes have been slower in the case of Caesareans. In the US in particular, mothers and babies may still be routinely separated. Read the section on gentle Caesareans in Chapter Three and inform your caregivers that immediate contact is essential to you, however, and your wishes should be carried out without undue resistance. You, the mother, have the power to change unhealthy routine practices that serve neither mother nor child.

It is possible, however, that after a C-section or highly medicalised birth a woman may not be able to interact immediately with her newborn; she may be nauseous or physically impaired. In this case, the baby's father or another birth companion can hold and soothe the baby until you are ready. If Dad is present, this is a great way to initiate bonding. With my last birth, after cuddling and feeding Alfie for the first half an hour after his birth, my husband took his shirt off and had a cuddle with him too, and reports this as the moment he fell irrevocably in love with our son. Including the father – and siblings or even grandparents too if you are having a home birth – helps the whole family unit to bond and support one another.

In many areas of the world, these practices are standard and have generally always been so. How did the Western world get it so wrong for so long?

Until the 1950s, the dominant theory of infant attachment was purely behavioural, which stated that babies only bonded the way they did with their mothers because their mothers fed them. It was purely a survival instinct and love had nothing to do with it. This was underpinned by Freud's theory of 'cupboard love' which he developed in the 1920s. This theory has also resulted in lots of detached parenting practices such as 'letting baby cry it out' and 'if you keep picking her up you'll spoil her', all of which have since been shown to be nonsense at best and detrimental at worst. In the 1950s John Bowlby, a child psychiatrist, formed his own theory of attachment, proposing that babies instantly seek not just food but also safety and physical and emotional security from their mother. Babies, he realised, are 'pre-programmed' to seek attachment and require attentive and responsive caregivers to thrive not just psychologically but physiologically too. Food was not enough. Babies need love and touch also. This has since been borne out in various studies. Now, we know that babies who have this immediate and natural time to bond with their mother during birth are significantly less stressed, sleep better, often find feeding easier and may even cry less. This is also a significant predictor in rates of postnatal depression.

Psychoanalysts and regression therapists now believe the baby experiences the birthing process in the following four stages, which have direct correlation to the stages of childbirth as a liminal experience (see Chapter One).

1. In utero. In late pregnancy your body and baby are getting ready for the birth. Your baby has had to become used to less freedom of movement and is now fixed in position for the birth. They have also become very aware of different noises and movements and are responsive to your physiology. Psychologically this is a time of expectancy and increased awareness and sensitivity as your baby prepares for the outside world. Staying as calm as possible in late pregnancy and using birth preparation techniques such as those described in Chapter Two will benefit your baby greatly at this stage. You can also use the bonding visualisation below.

2. Contractions start and baby experiences being compressed and pushed. This can be quite stressful, and so keeping relaxed and focused yourself will make it easier for your newborn.

3. Moving down the birth canal. Again the baby feels intense pressure and can become distressed if it goes on too long. Psychoanalysts term this a 'cataclysmic' experience. It's not hard to see why; your baby's whole world is literally changing!

4. Baby is born. This is often experienced in recalled memories as a 'rebirth' as baby moves from one world into the next. This can either be experienced as a frightening experience for baby that may have a lasting impact such as described above, or a joyful one where baby is 'reunited' with the mother, and you experience each other in a totally different way. Just as mothers often fall straight in love with their newborns, so does your newborn with you!

Lynne Murray, author of *The Social Baby*, identifies the period immediately after birth as setting the foundation for future interaction and communication. 'Newborn relatedness' is characterised by eye contact, touch, the sounds of the mother's voice and heartbeat which are familiar from in utero, and the mother's smell. Studies of newborns show that as well as a natural instinct to root for the breast, newborns will instinctively gaze at their mother and respond to her scent and voice.

To summarise then, the best ways to promote infant-mother attachment are:

- Immediate skin-to-skin contact.
- Quiet, undisturbed time together for at least an hour after birth, although other family members may be present to share in this.
- Initial breastfeeding.

Of course, there will be circumstances or emergency situations in which this isn't possible. We discussed in the last chapter ways to promote mother and baby interaction in the case of premature babies, but there may also be psychological barriers.

Some women, particularly those suffering from depression or birth trauma, worry they can't or won't bond with their baby. Using the information and resources in this book to have a positive birth experience will go a long way towards easing this. If, however, you do find immediate contact difficult – some women are in shock at the moment of birth and may need a few moments to register what has just happened! – have a birth partner or doula on hand to take the baby and then introduce you both when you are ready. This may be a great deal less stressful than feeling pressured into immediate contact if you really feel you can't manage it. Although your baby will of course prefer you as your smell is familiar, any warm and loving arms and gaze will provide her or him with the immediate comfort they need, and you can then take over in your own time. If you are having twins it may be too much to continually hold both babies after birth, so you and your partner could 'tag-team' in this way. You can also have your partner or companion hold the baby on your chest for you, which is sometimes a physically easier option after Caesarean.

If for any reason you don't get as much contact after birth with your baby as you would have wished, remember that birth is only one factor, albeit an important one, in both bonding and your child's development. You can substitute for this by:

- Having skin to skin as soon afterwards as you are able – talk to your caregivers and emphasise the importance of this.
- A rebirthing ritual as soon after the birth as you can in which you fully enjoy your sacred time 'after birth' with your baby.
- Having lots of cuddles, skin to skin and undisturbed time together in the days after the birth or when you bring baby home if they were premature – literally 'room in' with your baby. Visitors can wait.
- If you feel your baby has been affected by the birth, particularly if there was physical trauma such as forceps, you may want to consider taking them to a cranial osteopath who specialises in this. This has also been

shown to be effective in soothing colicky babies.

For pregnant first-time mothers bonding may also be a worry. When you have never experienced something before it can be difficult to imagine. This was certainly the case for me. During my first pregnancy, although I was excited and felt a vague sense of love for the new life inside me, I also felt sick, tired and scared. It all felt very surreal and I wondered when the intense feeling of motherhood I kept hearing about would arrive. What if it never did, I worried. What if I held my newborn son and felt nothing but confused and overwhelmed? Nothing prepared me for the rush of fierce, protective love that hit me when I finally held him, and you will most likely find this will be the case for you too, even if it doesn't happen immediately.

There are also things you can do to promote bonding during pregnancy. Rubbing your baby when you feel kicks and movement, singing and playing music to your bump, even talking to your bump, can all promote bonding and this in turn also can reduce perinatal depression. You can also try the following guided meditation. This is my own, but was inspired by the *yoga nidra* of Uma Dinsmore-Tuli. You will find a link to her work in the Resources section at the end of this chapter.

As with all the meditations and visualisations in this book, you can read and remember it, record on to a device and play back to yourself, or download it from: www.happybirthhappybaby. co.uk.

Exercise – Bonding With Your Baby

Just get yourself comfortable now... and now let your eyes find something on that wall... some spot or corner or a small object... and let your eyes rest on that point while you listen to the sound of my voice... hold your eyes open... and just look at that spot or that point... for a few moments... keep focusing on that spot... and your eyelids become heavy... heavier and heavier... blinking more and more... you can feel those eyelids becoming so heavy... but you just keep them open now... they may begin to water... that's okay... just keep them open... keep focusing... heavier and heavier... even though you want to close them you can keep them open for a few moments longer... and now close your eyes down... and as you close your eyes down you feel a wave of relaxation sweep through your entire body...

Now just focus on your breathing... breathing deeply... as you become so very deeply relaxed... breathing in... and breathing out... feeling your lungs and stomach expand as you breathe in... and your body relax so very deeply as you breathe out... relaxing more and more...

And now become aware of the quality of that relaxation... and imagine that relaxation spreading through the whole of your body... sweeping down from the top of your head to the tips of your toes... like a wave of relaxation... letting go... let go and relax every muscle in your body... that's right... really feel that relaxation from the crown of your head to the tips of your toes... feel how very good it feels to be this deeply relaxed...

Now bring your attention back to your breath... observe it flowing in and out through your nose... feel it in your throat... your chest... your belly... observe how your belly rises and falls along with your breath... and as you notice this... allow your breath to deepen and your belly to soften... imagine following your breath now as it runs through your body... and into your baby's body... you are breathing for your baby... breathing in... breathing out... sending oxygen to your baby... become aware of your heartbeat... and picture your baby in your womb... its own heart beating underneath yours... feel how you are so closely connected... breathing as one being... heartbeats creating a symphony with each other... your own unique beat... and spend a few moments just breathing and visualising... your baby and you... breath and heartbeat... you may like to place a hand on your belly... and send *love to your baby... smiling as you do so... letting your lips and jaw soften... and your breath just breathe itself naturally and easily...*

Now see your baby in your mind's eye... curled up safely and comfortably in your womb... nestling in your body... its home... its world... see your baby settling into position in your womb... getting ready to be born... ready to see you face to face... and picture your baby's face as it is now... its eyelids... its little nose... the softness of its cheeks... and lips... and chin... the soft round shape of its skull... and now take your attention down your baby's body... down each ridge and bump of its backbone... over its round belly... its arms and legs... count each little finger and thumb... each toe... see your baby, perfect and whole... this baby that you created and nurture and carry...

Bring your attention back to your chest now... to your heart... feel a warmth gathering there... and as you inhale increase this feeling... and as you exhale send it down into your womb to your baby... breathe in warmth... exhale it to your baby... breathe in love... exhale it to your baby... and continue in this way for a few minutes more.

(Pause here for a few minutes.)

Bring your attention back to your body now... feel where it meets the surface you are lying on... and become aware of the room around you... stretch your arms and legs lightly... and open your eyes when you are ready.

As we spoke about in the previous chapter, women who have given birth before may find themselves feeling guilty about not having had the 'perfect birth' with their previous children. It's important to remember that studies also show that children don't need 'perfect' parenting, but 'good enough' parenting. It's the same with birth. Although its endemic among mothers to worry they're not getting it right or to feel intense guilt about what they could have done better, the very fact that you're worrying shows you're probably doing just fine. I also can't reiterate enough that mothers are not responsible for the Westernised medical model of birth, and that we can't make informed choices when no one is informing us! Now, however, we have the chance to take this power back.

If you do have older children and you're worried their birth has affected them, the next section looks at the phenomenon of birth memories and how to bring healing when they are less than positive. This is also something you may well wish to apply to yourself; particularly if you were born before the early 90s you (and your mother) would be lucky to have had an unassisted birth. Unconscious birth trauma from our own births may affect how we feel around giving birth ourselves, so by working to heal this we can ensure we don't repeat the pattern – or pass it on to our daughters. When we look at the phenomenon of epigenetics later on, we will see that this is a very real possibility.

Birth Memories

Psychologists and psychotherapists have known about the effects of birth memories for some time. In 1988 an article was published in the *Journal of Prenatal and Perinatal Psychology and Health* that noted the growing evidence for birth memories and concluded they were of great significance for psychological outcomes. Although not all experts agree with this, the numbers of people recalling their own births, often while under hypnosis, are growing, and make more sense in light of the new research that shows us babies are born fully sentient and capable of communication and intimacy. Again, this is something mothers have known or intuitively suspected since dawn began, and only now is science catching up!

The research conducted in the 80s and onward found four dimensions to birth memories. These were:

- Clinical, or providing evidence for how a traumatic birth can lead to later psychological problems.
- Humanistic, illustrating how babies were affected at birth

by those around them.

- Holistic, indicating the interactions between feelings and physical sensations, right from birth.
- Transpersonal, or the sense that a power greater than ourselves is present.

From this it seems birth, and the unconscious memories we store from this time, can affect us on some profound levels. Of course, the notion of birth memory was strongly contended. Very few people remember in adulthood anything from before the age of three, because our long-term conscious memory wasn't formed. The hippocampus, the area of the brain largely responsible for this, is barely developed at birth. However, babies are born with a mature amygdala which is associated with implicit, emotional memory. This would explain why birth memories tend to resurface in dreams, altered states including illness, or under hypnosis. Many parents have been astounded when their older children recall things about their birth they could not possibly have known. There is also a great deal of anecdotal evidence of younger children recalling not just birth memories but their time in the womb. This is no longer so surprising now that we know babies are born programmed to respond to their mother's voice and heartbeat; sounds they heard while in the womb. If we can subconsciously remember the womb, why not birth?

Those who work with birth memories believe that unprocessed implicit memories of being born can contribute to stress-related diseases and anxiety in later life. This may particularly be the case where the mother was highly fearful during labour, causing her and her baby's system to be flooded with the stress hormone cortisol. Where there was prolonged separation from the mother there may be lingering feelings of not being good enough, fear of abandonment and of disconnection to others in the world. If feelings like this persist and there seems to be no other triggering event for them, it may well be that birth trauma and separation is the cause.

Birth memories rarely arise by themselves, but often resurface during dreams or regression therapy. Dream themes, according to psychoanalysis, that may indicate birth memories include:

- compression around the head
- tunnels – especially being trapped
- earthquakes
- tidal waves
- falling
- suffocation
- dreams that feel 'druggy'
- being paralysed, especially from the waist down

Of course dream interpretation is very subjective. Regression hypnosis is something that should be done face-to-face and so is beyond the scope of this book, but do seek out a practitioner in your local area if this is something you would like to explore.

The easiest way to find out if you have unprocessed birth memories is to ask, providing that is possible for you. If your birth involved any of the following, chances are it would benefit you to do some birth memory work.

- Assisted delivery, particularly if there was any physical trauma to you and your mother.
- A Caesarean.
- Periods where you or your mother were in distress; especially if she thought at any point that she or you were in danger.
- Prolonged separation from your mother after birth.
- Premature birth (including induction).
- Rough handling by medical staff.

To fully heal this type of trauma as an adult, a recently discovered and highly effective therapy is an advanced form of EFT known as Matrix Reimprinting, where the traumatic memory is accessed and EFT used to process and reframe it. Again, this is deep work that needs a practitioner in person. I recommend exploring the work of Sharon King, author of *Heal Your Birth, Heal Your Life*. Many hypnotherapists and regression therapists also specialise in traumatic birth imprints. Cranial osteopathy can release trauma that has been trapped in your body and is effective at any age.

For a gentle introduction to healing your own birth (deep trauma work is not recommended in pregnancy unless it is an urgent situation) you can try the following guided visualisation of my own, in which your adult self will embrace and soothe the baby you were. This can be very comforting. I would also suggest you try the Birth Journey visualisation in Chapter One.

If you have had any other major trauma or abuse in your past, particularly in childhood, please skip the following visualisation and seek a face-to-face session.

Exercise – Guided Visualisation for Healing Your Own Birth

Just get yourself comfortable now... and now let your eyes find something on that wall... some spot or corner or a small object... and let your eyes rest on that point while you listen to the sound of my voice... hold your eyes open... and just look at that spot or that point... for a few moments... keep focusing on that spot... and your eyelids become heavy... heavier and heavier... blinking more and more... you can feel those eyelids becoming so heavy... but you just keep them open now... they may begin to water... that's okay... just keep them open... keep focusing... heavier and heavier... even though you want to close them you can keep them open for a few moments longer... and now close your eyes down... and as you close your eyes down you feel a wave of relaxation sweep through your entire body...

Now just focus on your breathing... breathing deeply... as you become so very deeply relaxed... breathing in... and breathing out... feeling your lungs and stomach expand as you breathe in... and your body relax so very deeply as you breathe out... relaxing more and more...

And now become aware of the quality of that relaxation... and imagine that relaxation spreading through the whole of your body... sweeping down from the top of your head to the tips of your toes... like a wave of relaxation... letting go... let go and relax every muscle in your body... that's right... really feel that relaxation from the crown of your head to the tips of your toes... feel how very good it feels to be this deeply relaxed...

When you are ready I want you to imagine... in as much detail as is right for you now... a beautiful spiral staircase that takes you down to a special place... a safe place that is just for you... maybe the staircase has an ornate textured handrail, or maybe it is more plain and smooth, whatever is right for you now... either way it feels inviting to you and you go down... a step at a time... as I count from ten to one... and as I do so you can imagine yourself going down... a step at a time... going deeper and deeper... ten... nine... eight... see yourself going down... seven... six... hear your footsteps on the stairs, feel the stairs beneath your feet, and imagine yourself going deeper still... five... four... three... two... one... you step down and you can find yourself in your special place... and you can explore and take in all of the wonderful things there are to experience... all of the sights and sounds and smells... see what there is to see... feel what there is to feel... and just for a few moments take in all of the details of your special place... knowing that this safe place is just for you and you can return here whenever you choose...

Now you look up and you see a path in front of you... it curves into the distance and you cannot see what is round the corner... but you feel intrigued and a sense that you need to go down this path... and you do so, feeling a sense of curiosity... this curiosity grows...

along with a feeling of wonder... as you get closer towards that curve... you see scenes from your life flashing along the sides of the path... familiar scenes of everyday life... of family and friends... and you realise that you are walking backwards along your life... as you see yourself getting younger and younger in the scenes...

And you carry on along the path... watching your life unfold around you... taking you back to childhood... to toddlerhood... and just pause for a moment now and watch yourself... the child you were... feeling a deep sense of love and compassion for your younger self... remembering the simple curiosity and wonder of being a small child... and how new and fresh and exciting the world could be... and as you turn back to the path now you realise you are at the bend in the road you saw earlier... you pause for a moment... knowing something important is waiting... then taking a deep breath you follow the road round... and the path comes to an end... leaving a wild landscape beyond.

You stop, wondering where you are to go now... then hear a noise at your feet... you look down and see a newborn baby, wrapped in a blanket, whimpering softly... you reach down and pick her up, cradling the baby to your chest, feeling a wave of compassion flood you for this helpless, perfect little child... as you clasp the baby to your chest, rocking her gently... the whimpering stops and the baby's eyes meet yours, and you feel a rush of love... you take in the baby's features, her little nose and mouth... her soft cheeks... her beautiful eyes... and you realise that this baby is you... and you lift her up to nuzzle your face into her neck and whisper in her ear all the things you know she needs to hear... you tell her how loved she is... how safe she is... how you will always care for her and respond to her needs... she is so loved... you are so loved... and you feel her little body relax as she goes to sleep in your arms... knowing she is safe and protected and loved...

You turn round and make your way back up the path... cradling your baby self in your arms... and as you do so you see that the scenes from your life have gone and you are walking through a wood... you hear birds overhead and the sound of a stream nearby and you have a sense of safety and peace... and you continue through this wood... taking note of the colours and sounds and smells around you... your sense of safety and peace increasing... and the baby in your arms looks perfectly content... and you see a woman a little ahead of you on the path... facing you... and you know instinctively that she is good... and that she is waiting for you... and as you get closer you see that she looks like you... but older and wiser... and serenity radiates from her... and you know this is your Inner Guide, your Wise Self... and you can trust her to keep the baby in your arms safe and soothed... you give the baby a kiss on her perfect forehead and place her in the woman's arms... and the woman smiles at you kindly as she turns and walks away into the wood with the baby you... and you watch them go... knowing you can return to them any time you choose... return to this safe and serene place... and you feel a sense of release and freedom... and you continue on down the path... knowing a bright future awaits you...

And you can bring yourself back to your safe place now, ready to return to your waking life, knowing that you can bring these new feelings and new responses with you... and when you return you will return refreshed and alert.

Take a few more moments to enjoy your special place before you begin to wake up... feeling calm and refreshed... and you will begin to wake up as I count from one to five... fully refreshed... calm and alert... one... beginning to come up... two... becoming aware of the room around you... three... eyelids beginning to flicker... four... nearly there now... and five... OPEN YOUR EYES AND LOOK AROUND YOU, ALERT AND REFRESHED.

Healing your own birth or at least taking steps towards this may help you release any unconscious fears that are holding you back from giving birth confidently yourself, or help you clarify why certain events or situations are a big no-no for your birth plan.

I also believe that having a positive birth experience now

can also help go a long way towards healing any unconscious negative memories from your own birth. This is reflected in my own experience. You may recall from the Introduction that either an episiotomy or forceps would have been the very worst outcome for me. I now know as a birth practitioner that they are indeed better avoided, yet this doesn't explain my nearly phobic fear, even at the age of nineteen when I knew very little about birth. Only recently did my mother finally tell me that I was an assisted delivery and sustained cranial injuries, and that she was 'drugged up to the nines' as she puts it and completely disassociated from the entire event. I believe this explains my fears, and the despair I felt during my last birth when the obstetrician declared forceps were on the cards. I also believe the subsequent natural delivery after the midwife all but shooed the doctor out of the room was healing for me on so many levels. Not only was my son saved possible injury and a traumatic birth, but I believe this empowering experience healed my own. I believe that if we let it, birth can be a powerful healing as well as a transformative experience.

Resources/References

http://www.better-childbirth-outcomes.com/mother-baby-separation.html

https://evidencebasedbirth.com/can-hospitals-keep-moms-and-babies-together-after-a-cesarean

http://www.babycentre.co.uk/a658/bonding-after-birth

http://www.yonishakti.co/shop/yoga-nidra-5-nourishing-growth-nurturing-capacity-support-new-life-bhuvaneshwari

Heal Your Birth, Heal Your Life – Sharon King (Silverwood Books, 2015)

Chapter Six – BabyMoon

A new baby is like the beginning of all things – wonder, hope, a dream of possibilities.
Eda J. LeShan

So your baby is born. Once that incredible and life-changing reality has sunk in, the question in the back of most new mothers' minds is: what next? The physiological and psychological processes we've been talking about don't suddenly just end once the cord is cut (or drops off). There is a transition period, often referred to as the 'babymoon', where mother and baby get used to each other and their new world and feeding and bonding are established. Just like the Holy Hour after birth, this initial time, from around six weeks to the first three months (often referred to as the fourth trimester), is regarded in many cultures as sacred and vitally important.

Unfortunately, Western society promotes the 'yummy mummy' image, of the mother bouncing back into shape and her normal routines as quickly as possible, completely unchanged apart from the addition of a smiling, cooing baby on a perfectly toned hip. Not only is this completely unrealistic, chasing it is detrimental to both mother and baby. You've just given birth! A new life has been created! Things are forever changed, and a transition period to both assimilate these changes and find your own rhythm with your baby is not just advisable, it's necessary.

Of course, this will look different for every woman. Six weeks of lying around beatifically breastfeeding while your partner and the women of your family run around after you and do all the cooking and cleaning may be the ideal but is likely to be unrealistic in today's culture. Indeed, many women don't access the support they do have because of a need to be 'up and about' and feel they would go stir-crazy if they just lay around with their baby for the first two months. Nevertheless, adequate rest and relaxation is important if you want to fully recover and transition into your new role with ease.

It's important for your baby too. Remember your baby has spent their entire existence up to now inside of you and will still need to be as close to you as possible, especially at first. Skin-to-skin contact for at least a few hours a day through the first few days and weeks is going to be your newborn's idea of bliss, especially if she or he is feeding from you at the same time! All of the reasons we identified as to why this is crucial at birth apply here too. So don't feel you are in any way being 'lazy' by taking this time out; rather you're investing in your baby's future and your own well-being, which is just as important to your baby.

The first few weeks build on the birth and immediate aftermath to establish bonding and form the mother-infant dyad, or what's also known as the 'mother/baby rhythm'. This is a cyclical rhythm whereby you and your baby are attuned to each other, spend as much time together as possible and have your individual needs met when apart so that you come back together nourished and rested. In practical terms, this means you spend lots of time just cuddling and feeding baby, but also having breaks where baby is cared for by someone else while you rest, eat, pamper yourself or go for a gentle walk, or just have a well-needed cup of tea with a friend. When this rhythm is allowed to unfold naturally and in a relaxed way this tends to result in calmer babies, easier breastfeeding and less stressed mothers. This last is crucial. Research into postnatal depression and anxiety shows that where this continues there are knock-on effects on the infant's emotional and cognitive development, largely because the mother isn't as attuned to her baby's needs and is unable to respond to her baby's cues and signals appropriately. Rather than this being yet another stick to beat mothers with, this needs to be seen as a wake-up call to society that we need to provide adequate care and support for mothers just as much as for the baby. In the postnatal as much as the antenatal period, the two are, if not one, inextricably bound up in the dance of life together.

There are seven behaviours that contribute to establishing this rhythm of mother and child:

- keeping mum and baby together as much as possible immediately after birth and during the initial postnatal period
- frequent touch
- communication between mother and baby
- comforting the baby's
- being aware of baby'ies needs for touch and comfort; not dismissing these behaviours as 'spoiling'
- developing synchrony – this leads to
- developing predictable cycles of sleeping, waking and feeding

This all sounds at odds with popular practices such as 'controlled crying' and programs that promise to make your baby keep to a 4-hour routine, yet evidence shows that a more natural, physiological approach that focuses on fostering attachment and nourishment for both mother and infant is likely to result in better outcomes as described above. Also, I have never met a newborn that was able to tell the time! They only know when they are hungry or tired and want a cuddle. Rather than leading to 'spoiled' children, this approach actually fosters secure attachment and promotes emotional intelligence in children.

Your Post- Birth Plan

Your Post-Birth Plan Because every woman and her situation is different, it's a good idea to spend some time before the birth thinking about what you do and don't want for your babymoon, just as you did your birth. Practical considerations such as maternity and paternity leave, other children and pets, visitors etc can impact heavily on the quality of those early weeks so a little forward planning can only ever be a good thing. In an ideal situation your partner, mother, friend or combination of would be able to provide practical and emotional support while you concentrate on spending time with the baby. In other words: leave housework and cooking to someone else! You can even work out a rota as part of your plan, where for example Granny comes round in the afternoon to help prepare food or look after older children while Dad spends some quality time with baby and Mum gets a well-deserved bubble bath and sleep. Ask friends in advance if they can help out in this way and what time they have to spare; something as simple as bringing a pot of nutritious home-made food round once a week that can be frozen can be a Godsend, and more help than yet another congratulations card or baby trinket (not that those things aren't nice). Often people want to help but aren't sure how, so when people say, 'Do you need anything?' be honest and tell them what you really want is for someone to pop to the shops for milk and bread, help with the school run or hold the baby for half an hour so you can have a shower or a nap.

Visitors are certainly an issue to be considered. You are likely to be inundated with well-meaning guests and visitors, including family you only usually see at Christmas. Although some women enjoy the company, you are just as likely to see it as an intrusion or feel self-conscious about the fact you are still in your pyjamas. Rather than forcing yourself to get presentable and gritting your teeth through Great Aunt Rose's sage advice, don't be afraid to put your foot down beforehand about who, when and for how long. Discuss this with your partner and he can act as a welcome advocate. A simple 'Next week would be better, we're really tired right now/having some family time' will suffice. Most people will understand and if the rest are offended, it may sound harsh but they're really not that important right now; you and your baby are.

Exercise – Writing a Post-Birth Plan for Visitors

If you're worried about being bombarded with visitors and find it hard to say no, consider writing out a visiting plan and giving it to relevant family and friends in the last weeks of your pregnancy. You could use the following as a template:

We are honoured you want to share in our celebration and can't wait to introduce you to the newest member of the ____ family; however, it is important to us we have some family and quiet time after the birth. So we are asking you to help support us in the following ways:

- *Please call before visiting; don't drop-in unannounced*
- *Please don't be offended if we say no; we will rearrange!*
- *Please don't stay longer than…*
- *It would be a great help if you could make your own tea and coffee and clear up after yourselves.*
- *If you would like to give gifts, we would really appreciate*
- *home-cooked food, nappies…*

Once the flurry of visitors and well-wishers is over and paternity leave is coming to a close, many women start to worry about a lack of support and feel overwhelmed. The old adages of 'sleep when the baby sleeps' and 'don't do any more housework than strictly necessary' are as true as they ever were. If you feel you could do with an extra pair of hands, particularly if you have had a multiple birth, a difficult birth, have older children or a lack of family support or are a single mother, you may want to consider hiring a postnatal doula. She will provide practical help and support as well as a listening ear. As with birth doulas (many do both) Doula UK have an access fund if cost is an issue and many doulas new to the role will do non-profit work. For emotional support, groups like the National Childbirth Trust and Mums in Mind also offer befriending services for postnatal women who feel they could do with some company and someone to listen. Also ask your health visitor what is available in your area.

Feeding Your Baby

We all know breastfeeding is best for your baby. Like a natural birth, early breastfeeding helps seed the baby's microbiome and fosters attachment and bonding. The health benefits of breastfeeding are well documented, and the World Health Organization recommends babies are exclusively breastfed for at least the first six months, then breastfed alongside weaning for at least the first year. Breastfeeding is a wholly natural function that your body is designed to do, provides optimal nutrition for your baby and is free and always available.

So why do so few of us do it? Research shows that the majority of women in the West stop breastfeeding and switch to an alternative within the first few months, and a significant amount of women don't breastfeed at all.

As ever, individual mothers are often made to feel guilty and as if they are harming their child by their 'failure' to follow the WHO recommendations, but the truth is new mothers are often suffering from a lack of support and self-belief. Most of us born in the late twentieth century, before the recognition that 'breast is best', were fed formula milk and may have grown up never witnessing breastfeeding or regarding it as a normal and natural process. According to a friend's mother, in the Eighties 'only hippies breastfed.' Just because the powers-that-be have caught on to their mistake and headed in the other direction, it can take some time for the collective female psyche to adjust. As a result, many of us may feel slightly apprehensive about breastfeeding, worry we won't make enough to feed our precious bundles of joy and are faced with pressures such as going back to work, mothers who never breastfed and may feel dismissed (guilty) by our decision to do so, and male partners who feel disgruntled they can no longer view our breasts as their playthings. Some women also have psychological blockages to breastfeeding, particularly if they have been sexually abused in their past, an issue that mainstream healthcare often fails to address.

Just like birth, there is a need to reframe breastfeeding. Rather than it being a chore or something to be feared, feeding our babies is a natural process and a sacred one. Your body, your milk, is uniquely tailored for your child, and when women are given support and time and the pressures of the modern world are lifted, breastfeeding can be intensely pleasurable. See the Resource section for a link to an excellent article on the spirituality of breastfeeding. Before we look at some practical ways to make breastfeeding easier as well as alternatives to breastfeeding, I would like to share my own breastfeeding story with you.

My Breastfeeding Story

When I had my first son at nineteen, I didn't even consider breastfeeding. I had never witnessed it and internalised my own mother's and other female relatives' disgust towards it. I wasn't breastfed myself. Neither did my antenatal midwife give me any information. I gave my son the same formula milk everyone I knew used, and he was a happy and thriving baby. He then developed asthma at eighteen months, just as the mainstream public health drive was starting to gain momentum (this was in 2001), and I felt intense guilt that there may be a connection. When I had my daughter four years later, I was determined to breastfeed and at first found it very easy. She latched on easily and I didn't have any real issues with sore nipples or milk supply.

I did, however, suffer from a complete lack of support and was expected to return to my normal routines instantly, including going back to work. My plan had been to use a breast pump, but I found they just didn't work for me at all. Although I soldiered on until she was weaned, it went from being the easiest thing in the world to the hardest. I was also struggling with postnatal depression.

Twelve years later, pregnant again and in very different circumstances with a lot more history and knowledge behind me,

I made the decision that I would mix feed, giving my son primarily breast milk supplemented with an organic formula alternative we chose after some detailed research. While I would never recommend this to another woman as an alternative to full breastfeeding, it worked for us as a family, by allowing my husband to be involved with some of the feeding and by taking the pressure off me. Because I felt I was making an empowered choice, taking my baby's needs into account without sacrificing my own, I sailed through the whole experience. Although there were brief periods where he started refusing the breast and preferring the bottle, I got around this simply by keeping on offering him the breast until he decided he liked it again; and in the meantime adding breast milk to his baby rice and oats so he was still taking in some of its goodness. Although there were a few times during these periods when I thought my milk would 'dry up' it soon returned in abundance! Nature has a way of working things out, if you let Her.

My experiences have left me a passionate supporter of both breastfeeding and also of supporting women and their choices.

If you want to breastfeed but have concerns about practicalities, make a plan for these in your Post-Birth Plan. Most women do get on well with breast pumps and there are more alternatives out there today. Find out what local support is available in your area in advance; you may well be surprised by the wealth of resources available to you, from NHS Lactation Supporters to NCT and La Leche Groups. If you have never had successful breastfeeding modelled for you, ask if you can go along to a few of these groups while you are still pregnant; observe and talk to the other women. Find out what breastfeeding friendly cafes and community centres are in your area. Consider hiring a postnatal doula who is also trained in breastfeeding support.

Also, when you are breastfeeding you can use the mindfulness and relaxation exercises in this book to really 'tune in' to the experience and your baby, and this will help calm any anxiety which is often at the root of minor problems. Try recording the relaxation below too. I have kept this light so it shouldn't induce sleep or too deep a state; nevertheless you're likely to be tired as a new mum and grateful for every forty winks so don't listen to this unless you are lying in a safe place with your baby (no sofas) or there is someone in the room with you.

Exercise – Relaxation for Promoting Breastfeeding

Get comfortable now and focus on your breathing... breathing deeply... as you become so very deeply relaxed... breathing in... and breathing out... feeling your lungs and stomach expand as you breathe in... and your body relax as you breathe out... relaxing more and more... just enough to feel calm and still... but still aware of everything around you...

And now become aware of the quality of that relaxation... and imagine that relaxation spreading through the whole of your body... sweeping down from the top of your head to the tips of your toes... like a wave of relaxation... letting go... let go and relax every muscle in your body... that's right... really feel that relaxation from the crown of your head to the tips of your toes... feel how very good it feels to be this relaxed...

Concentrate on the feeling of your baby at your breast now, simply being present and observing the feelings and sensations that occur... while remaining in this state of light and complete relaxation...

Watch your baby... observing every detail of his/her little body, their mouth suckling at your breast and the feeling of contentment on their face as they do so... watch yourself feeding your baby... nourishing your baby... knowing what a sacred exchange this is... while simply observing the flow of feelings and sensations that happens as your baby feeds from your breasts...

Think about how your body is uniquely designed to do this... how your body instinctively knows how to feed and nourish your child... and be aware of being part of this process... visualise the

*milk as it is made in your breasts and flows into your child...
nurturing... promoting growth and health... and as you breathe
slowly and deeply become aware of the flow of your milk and rhythm
of your baby's suckling... and imagine as you breathe in these warm
feelings of calm and soothing you breathe them out into your baby
along with your milk... feeding your baby love and nourishment...
and just breathe this way for a few moments.* (Pause here for as
long as you wish.)

*Just relax here for a few moments... and when you are ready
or your baby stops feeding stretch your limbs and have a drink of
water... feeling alert, relaxed and refreshed.*

There are sometimes medical or psychological barriers to
breastfeeding, or you may have to take a medication that is
incompatible with breastfeeding. If this is the case, or if you decide
breastfeeding isn't the right decision for you, don't beat yourself
up. Instead, look into the alternatives and make an informed choice
about what is best for you and your baby. After all, the bottom line
is that your baby gets fed and thrives! And you may find you have
more choices than you thought.

Standard formula milks have to conform to certain standards
and all should provide adequate nutrition. You may prefer to
choose an organic or even dairy-free formula. I would suggest
talking to an infant nutritionist and also to other mums.

There are two options you may not have thought of: making
your own formula, or using another woman's breast milk.
Both are becoming more and more popular and therefore more
accessible. There are many recipes around for infant formula, so
I would suggest ensuring that whichever you use is approved
by an infant nutritionist and, as ever, do your research. You may
have noticed I use that phrase a lot! That's because, as well as the
importance of knowing you have choice, I believe the best expert
on her own baby is the mother, and it's important to weigh up
your options and go with your own knowledge and opinion

than simply follow the party line. I have provided a link to a reputable source below which will help get you started if you want to explore this avenue.

Milk banks and milk sharing is also becoming more possible, so there may well be a 'milk bank' in your area in which you can obtain breast milk for your baby. If this seems strange to you, remember that for centuries many women used 'wet nurses' to feed their children. This may be an ideal solution for women who want their babies to have breast milk but have medical reasons why they can't feed their babies themselves. It's also a great alternative for adoptive parents.

Your Newborn's Wish List

I'm not a believer in prescriptive 'how to' parenting, but there are a few general things that babies universally tend to love and which all promote bonding, calm and optimal development. If you do feel you would like the advice of an expert or to join a parenting group, I believe Baby Calm, founded by Sarah Ockwell Smith, is fantastic for promoting the mother-baby rhythm and helping parents make the transition into their new life with their infant.

These are likely to be high on your baby's wish list:

- Being carried. Babies would happily be held at all times in the early weeks. Because this isn't always practical, think about investing in a good quality sling; although this is now popularly known as 'babywearing' and is becoming a movement in attachment parenting circles, it is a practice that is as old as the hills. Although you can find all kinds of modern-looking fiddly harnesses a traditional sling is often more comfortable and a lot easier to wear!
- Co-sleeping. Your health visitor will advise you that your baby should only sleep in their own bed, on their back, but co-sleeping is becoming more and more popular as

research shows the benefits for both mother and baby. In terms of safety, it's generally no riskier than sleeping in their own bed providing neither you nor your partner smoke, have been drinking or taking anything, you don't use duvets or pillows near your baby or loose bedding, and you make sure there are no gaps your baby can get stuck in. If the idea of bed sharing makes you uncomfortable, you can buy a co-sleeping crib which attaches to your bed so providing safety while keeping your baby close.

- White noise. Perhaps because it sounds similar to the inside of the womb, many parents report their infants fall asleep within minutes of hearing white noise. There are lots of downloads and free videos available on YouTube which will provide hours of white noise. Recently enjoying popularity is 'pink noise' which is a similar frequency and which babies also seem to love.

- Movement. Again, it may remind them of being carried in the womb, as most infants love being rocked and carried. Patting them rhythmically on the back is an instinctual thing people seem to do when holding a baby (and not just to produce a burp!); this likely reminds them of your heart beating above them in utero.

- You. Your touch, your smell, your voice, the sound of your heartbeat and lots of smiles and eye contact. Fresh out of the womb, to a newborn the mother is still Home.

Mother Warming

Becoming a mother is a major transition, and even if it isn't your first child, the same applies. After all you have never mothered this child before and the new addition will signal a change in family dynamics and your day to day routine just as much as a first baby. Often in Western culture the need to mark and honour this transition is largely forgotten and ignored, although postnatal rituals are finally coming back into favour along with traditional birth practices.

You can find different variations of postnatal rituals around the world but they all have similar themes: that of saying goodbye to the woman you were before this birth and greeting and blessing the woman you are now. Another is that of keeping the new mother warm, both literally, energetically and nutritionally. After birth we have lost a lot of energy, blood and nutrients and mother warming is all about replenishing these and giving ourselves some rest and care. There are many women's wellness therapists who now offer mother warming treatments, which usually consist of a range of holistic therapies, herbal and nutritional remedies. At my own clinic I offer postnatal massage, belly-wrapping (which helps the muscles and pelvic bones heal and stabilise), herbal treatments and nutritional recipes. You can also find traditional practitioners who will offer a 'Closing the Bones' ceremony, a traditional postnatal ceremony for mothers that involves mourning the old life and embracing the new, using movement techniques designed to help restabilise the pelvic floor. I have written a guided visualisation below based around the idea of transitioning from the old life to the new which you may like to try, recording and playing back to yourself or downloading from the website. This will relax you deeper than the breastfeeding relaxation so make sure someone else is watching the baby and take a few moments out just for you, making sure you are wrapped up nice and warm.

Placenta remedies are also believed to provide much-needed nourishment after the birth. If cooking your placenta or popping it in a smoothie isn't up your street, you can freeze it and pay for it to be encapsulated and take it as you would a vitamin. Ingesting the placenta is a relatively new phenomenon that is rapidly gaining in popularity.

Whatever you go for, I strongly suggest you take some time out for self-care and nurture during this transitional time. Remember – a happy, healthy mama is a happy, healthy baby!

Exercise – Stepping into Your New Life Visualisation

Just get yourself comfortable now... and now let your eyes find something on that wall... some spot or corner or a small object... and let your eyes rest on that point while you listen to the sound of my voice... hold your eyes open... and just look at that spot or that point... for a few moments... keep focusing on that spot... and your eyelids become heavy... heavier and heavier... blinking more and more... you can feel those eyelids becoming so heavy... but you just keep them open now... they may begin to water... that's okay... just keep them open... keep focusing... heavier and heavier... even though you want to close them you can keep them open for a few moments longer... and now close your eyes down... and as you close your eyes down you feel a wave of relaxation sweep through your entire body...

Now just focus on your breathing... breathing deeply... as you become so very deeply relaxed... breathing in... and breathing out... feeling your lungs and stomach expand as you breathe in... and your body relax so very deeply as you breathe out... relaxing more and more...

And now become aware of the quality of that relaxation... and imagine that relaxation spreading through the whole of your body... sweeping down from the top of your head to the tips of your toes... like a wave of relaxation... letting go... let go and relax every muscle in your body... that's right... really feel that relaxation from the crown of your head to the tips of your toes... feel how very good it feels to be this deeply relaxed...

And as deep as you are now... you can go ten times deeper. In a moment I am going to ask you to open your eyes... and then when you close them again you will go ten times deeper... so very deeply relaxed... relaxed in body and mind...

When you are ready I want you to imagine... in as much detail as is right for you now... a stone staircase that takes you down to a special place... a safe place that is just for you... it feels inviting to you and you go down... a step at a time... as I count from ten to one... and as I do so you can imagine yourself going down... a step at a time... going deeper and deeper... ten... nine... eight... see yourself going down... seven... six... hear your footsteps on the stairs, feel the stairs beneath your feet, and imagine yourself going deeper still... five... four... three... two... one... you step down and you can find yourself in your special place... and you can explore and take in all of the wonderful things there are to experience... all of the sights and sounds and smells... see what there is to see... feel what there is to feel... and just for a few moments take in all of the details of your special place... knowing that this safe place is just for you and you can return here whenever you choose...

Take a few moments to enjoy your special place and when you are ready now you see a path opening up in front of you through a forest and it looks inviting to you so you begin to walk along it... feeling the ground underneath your feet and the warm bright sun above you... you can hear birdsong and smell the scent of flowers in bloom... you become aware of the sound of running water and see a stream alongside the path, with crystal clear water... you carry on walking... and soon become aware of a small boat gliding up alongside you on the stream at the side of the path... you turn and see a woman in the boat... and you see that this woman is you... as you were before... before the birth... before the baby grew in your womb... and you know she has some things to say to you before you wish her goodbye and so you step into the boat and sit opposite her and you both continue down the stream...

And for a few moments while you no longer hear the sound of my voice you talk to this former you... telling her everything that you will miss about her... and learning from her all the wisdom you need to take forward from her...

(Pause for a few moments while you engage in this inner dialogue.)

And you are ready now to get out of the boat and walk forward into your new life... so you lean forward to embrace her and as you both say goodbye she gives you a gift... a gift that symbolises all the experience she has to give you that will help you in your new life... and you thank her and turn and step out of the boat and back on to the path... and you watch her drift back down the stream the way she had come until she disappears from view... and you turn and walk up the path again... feeling free and strong and empowered and fully ready to embark on your new life with your baby... knowing that you have everything you need... all the inner resources you need...

And you can bring yourself back to your body and your breath now, ready to return to your waking life, knowing that you can bring these new feelings and new responses with you... and when you return you will return refreshed and alert.

Take a few more moments to enjoy this relaxation before you begin to wake up... feeling calm and refreshed... and you will begin to wake up as I count from one to five... fully refreshed... calm and alert... one... beginning to come up... two... becoming aware of the room around you... three... eyelids beginning to flicker... four... nearly there now... and five... OPEN YOUR EYES AND LOOK AROUND YOU, ALERT AND REFRESHED.

Resources/References

http://www.better-childbirth-outcomes.com/mother-baby-rhythm.html

https://talkbirth.me/2012/06/25/breastfeeding-as-a-spiritual-practice/

http://www.nhs.uk/conditions/pregnancy-and-baby/pages/breastfeeding-help-support.aspx

Ina May's Guide to Breastfeeding – Ina May Gaskin (Bantam, 2009)

The Womanly Art of Breastfeeding – La Leche League International (Ballantine Books, 2010)

The Politics of Breastfeeding – Gabrielle Palmer (Pinter & Martin, 2009)

https://wellnessmama.com/53999/organic-baby-formula-options/

http://hm4hb.net/

http://www.calmfamily.org/

http://babycalmblog.com/index.html

https://babywearinginternational.org/

https://www.nct.org.uk/parenting/co-sleeping-safely-your-baby

http://www.tyckledtales.com/2012/12/03/postpartum-recovery-care-new-mom/

https://placentaremediesnetwork.org/placenta-encapsulation/

Part Three – Happy Birth, Happy World

To change the world, we must first change the way babies are being born.
Michel Odent

Chapter Seven – Giving Birth to the Future

When a human is born, they're already filled with intuitive knowledge of centuries and centuries of people before them. A child has wisdom. Their cells have wisdom.
Bruce Lipton

At the beginning of this book I stated that changing birth can change the world. It's not just a cute strapline.

So far we have looked at how birth can be personally transformative, and how it has far-reaching effects on the well-being of both mother and baby, even extending far into baby's future and setting the foundation for both future health, and emotional and cognitive functioning. It is a natural step to conclude that, by having an effect on the well-being of the people that make up our social world, so that world will change. When I examined that conclusion in more detail, what I discovered was fascinating.

And it doesn't end there. In this chapter we will look at four interlinked areas in which how we birth is shaping our society and our world. Human rights issues, evolution of humanity, ecology and even spirituality are all shaped by our birth practices, our beliefs about birth and women's agency to birth the way they choose. Pretty mind-blowing!

Each of these topics deserves a book by themselves, so I can only give a brief overview here which I hope will whet your appetite to find out more or, at the very least, increase your confidence to make the birth choices that are right for you. There are exercises at the end of each section that I hope will bring this information 'down to earth' and help you think about these areas in ways that are personal to you and your baby.

Human Evolution

It almost sounds far-fetched, doesn't it, that the way we birth can affect the evolution of humankind? Yet the cumulative effects of changing birth are being shown to do this very thing. There has been much recent speculation that higher rates of C-sections are leading to babies being bigger as they are less likely to be restricted by the birth canal. This taken to its logical conclusion means Caesareans could become the 'normal' way to give birth. So far the cultural and medical changes modern society has imposed upon childbirth has had negative consequences as we shall see, yet as women begin to reclaim their births (and evidence-based science is increasingly backing them in this) this pattern can be changed. The recent recognition of the importance of skin-to-skin contact, for example, and delayed cord clamping could increase physiological and psychological well-being in the next generation and those to come.

Michel Odent (yes, him again) is a big believer on the impact of the medicalisation of birth on human evolution, and one of the topics he has done extensive research on involves oxytocin and its replacement with drugs in a medicalised birth. We have seen how crucial oxytocin is for birth and bonding with the baby, so what happens when our very beginnings are deficient in 'love hormones'? Do we become less loving?

Odent and others believe so. If, as we saw in Chapter Five, the foundations for interactions with others are laid down at birth, then when these interactions are interrupted or characterised by stress hormones rather than the calm and connection response, we're setting the stage for generations of people with less ability to connect with others. Less empathy. Less love. Odent believes we can trace the evolution of aggressive behaviour in humans alongside the changes from natural birth practices. This may have resulted in greater technological and economic advances, but at what cost?

Narcissism is on the rise, whether that be evident in the

showboating of world leaders at the expense of the people they are sworn to serve, or the selfie craze our teens are obsessing about. Particularly in the West where medicalised childbirth is the norm, we are becoming ever more selfish – me, me, me – and ever more focused on consumption – more, more, more. Narcissism, psychopathy and sociopathy are characterised by lack of empathy and lower oxytocin levels. According to birth researchers, this is far from a coincidence.

Of course, I'm not suggesting that just because a baby isn't born in optimal conditions he or she is going to grow up to become a megalomaniac; nevertheless it is interesting to see what happens to collective trends when women and babies' innate needs are bypassed in favour of technology and fear-based assumptions.

We see a similar pattern in the case of birth trauma contributing to postnatal depression, which then may increase the baby's chance of having cognitive and emotional disorders in later life. In so many areas, the increasing medicalisation of birth is having a negative impact on who we are becoming as a species. If this continues, we may well see a time when oxytocin is naturally no longer released during the birthing and bonding process.

That all sounds pretty depressing, I know, but there is a lot of reason for optimism. As awareness of these issues increases, as women around the world start to say 'no more' and birth their way, this never needs to happen. Instead we can create a world where, whatever type of birth a woman has, the focus is on natural oxytocin, the calm and connection response and meeting the needs of mothers and babies. Research shows that babies born in a loving environment into a loving pair of arms will actually have more oxytocin receptors in their brain. This means a greater capacity for love. In this way, the next generation may not be another 'generation of narcissists' but rather be pioneers of a more compassionate, loving and equal society. And it all begins with birth!

Childbirth affects us on a genetic level. Just as our genes influence our behaviour, so the recent science of epigenetics shows us that our behaviour affects our genes; and therefore the genes of our descendants. Epigenetics literally means 'on top of' genetics and refers to modifications of existing DNA which cause, to put it very crudely, specific gene expressions to be turned 'on' or 'off'. Our environments can cause epigenetic changes and lead to differences in our characteristics. Early environment, including in utero, birth and infancy, can lead to long-term epigenetic changes. These can then be inherited. So when someone comments you have a temperament very like the grandmother you never met, we can now understand how that does in fact happen. Epigenetics also explains how that can change over the course of your lifetime.

Professor Soo Downe, who has been awarded an OBE for her contribution to midwifery and childbirth practices, has begun conducting research into how birth practices affect oxytocin receptors in the brain and how, through epigenetic processes, these changes can then be inherited. So far such studies are proving Odent's theory. How we birth can affect who we become.

Unless you're a scientist, the details of this new research can be hard to take in, so I won't go any further here (not least because I'd be out of my depth). Nevertheless as a birth practitioner and mother I find this topic fascinating, and also empowering. Collectively, when not interfered with by cultural bias or trauma, the natural instincts of a birthing woman are to give birth in privacy, in a nurturing environment with loving companions and get into her birthing zone. Left alone, mothers and babies naturally gravitate towards immediate bonding processes like skin-to-skin contact. These instincts have been ignored and denigrated for so long and yet now here they are, coming into centre stage as science shows again and again that the real experts on the birth process are those experiencing it. It's time to take our power back.

We just need to believe it. Bruce Lipton, a pioneer in the field of epigenetics, has discovered that it isn't just environment and behaviour that affect our genes, it is also our beliefs.

The idea that our thoughts shape our reality is nothing new and has been the subject of spiritual and New Age discussion for some time, but what Lipton is talking about is more concrete than that. Our beliefs, the internal maps we make of the world, *the stories we tell ourselves*, actually alter our gene expression. Our biology. And therefore evolution.

How does that affect childbirth? We've come almost full circle here to where we began: discussing how the way we think about childbirth can determine the way we experience it. More than that, the way our mothers, grandmothers and our entire cultures think about childbirth affects the way we experience it. Decades if not centuries of women being made to feel they couldn't give birth without medical intervention has resulted in just that. Some researchers believe the inevitable conclusion to this is all babies being born by Caesarean section, and the power of birth as we know it being lost to us forever. Do I believe that? No, I believe it's a possibility, but I also think the tide has already turned, and we are on our way to the more optimistic vision I spoke about earlier.

The best way to achieve that vision is to believe we can.

I have given exercises for changing our beliefs about birth in the first three chapters, but something we haven't looked at yet is affirmations. The idea of changing our beliefs with affirmations has also been around for a long time, but I have found when working with women that we can be very resistant to this. This is likely to be because consciously saying something to ourselves that we know we don't believe just feels too false. The trick with affirmations is to use them while in a more receptive state, so they are heard by our subconscious – which is where the change happens. For this reason affirmation done under hypnosis or as part of a therapy such as EFT can be very effective. You can use hypnosis techniques on yourself to achieve light relaxation, as the exercise below shows, before you say your affirmations. This is a common technique in hypnobirthing.

Exercise – Relax Yourself

There are a variety of ways you can guide yourself into a more receptive state which will make you more receptive to your affirmations and therefore help you change your beliefs at the cellular level. Try the following and see which ones work for you, or you can use them all in sequence for maximum effect. I would recommend at least one of the body scan or breath exercises followed by one of the countdowns.

Active Body Scan
Lie or sit comfortably and take a few deep breaths. You are going to consciously squeeze and release your muscles, one muscle group at a time. Start with your head and move down to your toes. Squeeze each muscle group as hard as you can on the inhale, then breathe out and release, feeling how the muscles feel more relaxed than before. By the time you get to your toes, your whole body will be deeply relaxed.

Visualisation Body Scan
Lie or sit comfortably and take a few deep breaths. Now visualise a warm light in your favourite colour at the top of your head and see it slowly travel down your whole body, until your entire body is filled with this warm, relaxing light. Keep your breathing deep and slow, making your exhale slightly longer than your inhale.

Heart/Womb Breathing
Lie or sit comfortably and take a few deep breaths. Bring your attention to your heart area and imagine you are breathing into and out of your heart area. Feel your chest rising and falling, keep

your breathing deep and calm. You may like to breathe into your womb instead, fostering a feeling of connection with your baby. Or you can combine the two by inhaling into your heart and exhaling into your womb.

Visualisation Countdown

Lie or sit comfortably and take a few deep breaths. Imagine a set of stairs in front of you, and count down from ten to one, seeing yourself take a step with each count. Set the intention that you will go deeper into relaxation with each step and by the time you have finished the countdown you will be completely calm, relaxed and receptive.

Mudra Countdown

Sit cross-legged and take a few deep breaths. Put your hands together in a prayer position in front of you, level with your forehead. As you count slowly down from ten to one bring your hands slowly down the front of your body until they are resting in your lap. Set the intention that you will go deeper into relaxation with each number and by the time you have finished the countdown you will be completely calm, relaxed and receptive.

Exercise – Birth Affirmations

Now repeat your affirmations while you are calm and relaxed. You can use the traditional technique of saying them to yourself in the mirror if this works for you, or simply say them slowly out loud, paying attention to the sound of the words as they come out of your mouth.

I have given some suggestions for affirmations below, however, it is always best that they are as personal to you as possible so adapt them as you wish. Keep them simple, positive and focused on what you do want, not what you don't. You also may like to write them down and stick them around where you can see them, or if you are feeling creative you could make your own birth affirmation cards (you can also buy these with generic affirmations on). These relaxation techniques followed by affirmations can be used during the birth itself, especially earlier on, but change any 'I will' statements to 'I am'.

Some suggestions for affirmations:

- *I am one with my baby. Me and my baby are calm and at peace. I know all will be well.*
- *My body is perfectly designed for birth. My body is perfectly designed for my baby.*
- *I love my baby and my baby feels this love and is calm and relaxed inside me.*
- *My birth will be a positive and amazing experience.*
- *My body knows how to birth my baby. I know how to birth my baby.*
- *I am strong. I am calm. I am relaxed.*
- *I will birth my baby from a place of love and strength. I have everything I need.*
- *My body is the expert in my baby's birth.*

Human Rights Issues

The way birth is handled is a human rights issue. We will look at some of the global pioneers of the woman-centred birth movement in the next chapter, so here I will just sketch out the background to this topic and invite you to explore how you feel about it.

Across the world, to varying degrees, women suffer human rights abuses in childbirth. Although in the developed world childbirth tends to be safer in terms of mortality and morbidity, we have seen that both women and babies in the West are suffering from the effects of traumatic birth, which is all too often contributed to by a basic lack of compassion and respect from medical staff.

The White Ribbon Alliance was set up in 1999 due to the efforts of independent midwife Theresa Shaver, who went on to train with a traditional midwife in Mauritania and then took her skills to Ethiopia. She then returned to the US to find that, although far more privileged than Ethiopia in terms of technology and living standards, human rights abuses in childbirth were no less prevalent. The WRA now campaign and work towards respectful maternity care across the globe.

The White Ribbon Charter developed the groundbreaking Respectful Maternity Care Charter in 2011. It sets out the following as a global framework for disrespect in maternity care:

- Physical Abuse – this includes rough handling of mother or baby and poorly performed procedures
- Non-Consented Care – care given without informed consent
- Non-Confidential Care
- Non-Dignified Care
- Discrimination – on grounds of socio-economic status, race, sexuality or gender-identification, disability, weight etc
- Abandonment of Care
- Financial Harassment

To look at this in terms of what we do want, the exact opposites are mapped out in the Charter as the seven fundamental rights of childbearing women:

- Freedom from harm
- Respect for preference and choice
- Right to privacy
- Right to dignity
- Freedom from prejudice and discrimination
- Equal access to care
- Freedom from coercion

In 2013 the Department of Health in the UK spoke about the '6Cs' that all medical caregivers should exercise: Care, Compassion, Competence, Communication, Courage and Commitment. Organisations such as Birthrights and global midwifery coalitions campaign to make these standard across maternity services.

Exercise – Journaling Questions – What Does This Mean to You?

Get out your notebook or journal and think about the following questions. Look at the seven fundamental rights listed above. What do they mean for you? What would you personally consider a violation of your rights? For example, feeling coerced into regular vaginal examinations that you find traumatic would violate at least five of these. You might feel it's a violation of your rights to be told you can't have a home birth as there are no local midwives available to attend. You might find certain language that your caregivers typically use as discriminatory or resonant of coercion.

Now think about the six 'Cs'. What do these words signify for you? How in your personal circumstances could a caregiver provide these for you?

Note these things and then have a look at the birth plan you wrote in Chapter Two. Do you want to make these things clearer? Or add anything?

Don't be afraid to exercise your rights. Thankfully the majority of us in the West are able to have a voice. We have already seen how important it is for your well-being and your baby's to have a right to choose your own birth. And it might help you to know that every time you exercise your freedom of choice – and speak out if it is violated – you are contributing to a global cause for the empowerment of all birthing women.

If you are interested in learning more about this subject, I strongly recommend you watch the documentary *Freedom for*

Birth by Toni Harman and Alex Wakeford.

Ecology and Birth

Deep Ecology aims to help us restore as a species what is undoubtedly a broken relationship with nature. In so many ways we live out of sync with the natural rhythms of our bodies and our world, behaving as though we are somehow independent of the Earth, forgetting that we too are part of the ecosystem. We no longer live in accordance with seasonal rhythms, which can result in problems such as Seasonal Affective Disorder as we try to carry on as usual during the winter months instead of obeying our bodies' calls for warmth and rest. We do a similar thing with our menstrual cycle; insisting on pretending it's not happening and living like a tampon ad instead of responding to the pain and tiredness and need for social withdrawal. It's no coincidence that PMS is a Western epidemic. I'm sure I don't need to draw the parallels to the way the developed world treats Planet Earth itself, with a total lack of disregard for the harm our rabid consumption in the West can cause. We see the same pattern yet again in the way the birth process, so cleverly designed by nature, has been co-opted and altered by modern technology.

When we reclaim physiological birth we reclaim our part in the ecosystem, putting ourselves in harmony with it rather than opposing it. Evidence-based research tells us that allowing the birth process to unfold as naturally as possible promotes greater health and well-being in both mother and baby. As we explored at the beginning of this chapter, this has knock-on effects on humanity as a whole. From an ecological perspective this benefits not just humanity but the entire ecosystem.

If we take this further, women become a microcosm of Nature itself, individual Mama Earths creating, gestating and birthing. Many women during pregnancy report feeling 'at one' with all things, more drawn to nature and animals (often on the other side animals are also drawn towards pregnant women, with the family dog for example suddenly becoming extra attentive and protective). Seeing your pregnancy and birth in this way can be encouraging for women who are feeling thoroughly fed up about the physical downsides of pregnancy, or have the sense they are doing something sacred and special and feel dismissed by a culture that values other things. If either of these are you, you may like to try the guided journey below.

In terms of birth practices, taking an ecological perspective has led researchers to coin the term 'biodynamic birthing' as the optimal way to birth for both safety and health. Although a natural physiological birth is always the goal, there are times intervention is both necessary and the most compassionate thing to do. Also in developing countries where levels of public health are poor, introducing modern birth practices can reduce both infant and maternal mortality. Biodynamic birthing aims to combine the best of all worlds, blending traditional birthing wisdom with evidence-based medical advances and compassionate, woman-centred care. There is an emphasis on working with natural rhythms of birth, and relationships rather than hierarchy between caregivers.

Often birth can bring a woman 'home' to both her body and its place in nature. There can be no denying the power of natural forces when feeling the surge of contraction waves, or crowning, or the intense joy that can come over a mother on holding her baby in her arms for the first time.

Exercise – Your Womb as Universe Visualisation

Just get yourself comfortable now... and now let your eyes find something on that wall... some spot or corner or a small object... and let your eyes rest on that point while you listen to the sound of my voice... hold your eyes open... and just look at that spot or that point... for a few moments... keep focusing on that spot... and your eyelids become heavy... heavier and heavier... blinking more and more… you can feel those eyelids becoming so heavy… but you just keep them open now… they may begin to water… that's okay… just keep them open… keep focusing… heavier and heavier… even though you want to close them you can keep them open for a few moments longer… and now close your eyes down… and as you close your eyes down you feel a wave of relaxation sweep through your entire body…

Now just focus on your breathing… breathing deeply… as you become so very deeply relaxed… breathing in… and breathing out… feeling your lungs and stomach expand as you breathe in… and your body relax so very deeply as you breathe out… relaxing more and more…

And now become aware of the quality of that relaxation… and imagine that relaxation spreading through the whole of your body… sweeping down from the top of your head to the tips of your toes… like a wave of relaxation… letting go… let go and relax every muscle in your body… that's right… really feel that relaxation from the crown of your head to the tips of your toes… feel how very good it feels to be this deeply relaxed…

And as deep as you are now… you can go ten times deeper. In a moment I am going to ask you to open your eyes… and then when you close them again you will go ten times deeper… so very deeply relaxed… relaxed in body and mind…

When you are ready I want you to imagine… in as much detail as is right for you now… a stone staircase that takes you down to a special place… a safe place that is just for you… it feels inviting to you and you go down… a step at a time… as I count from ten to one… and as I do so you can imagine yourself going down… a step at a time… going deeper and deeper… ten… nine… eight… see yourself going down… seven… six… hear your footsteps on the stairs, feel the stairs beneath your feet, and imagine yourself going deeper still… five… four… three… two… one… you step down and you can find yourself in a cave… it is warm… and the stone walls all around you glow a soft, welcoming red… you get the impression that you are both inside your own womb and deep inside the centre of the Earth at the same time... and you just stop for a moment to enjoy this place... feeling safe and supported... nurtured and loved... and you become aware of a pulse beneath your feet... like a heartbeat... which seems to rise up through your body... through your veins... merging with the beating of your heart... just listen to this sound... the pulse of life... feeling yourself merge with the creative power of the Earth and even the universe itself... you feel a warm glow in your chest and it gives you strength, calm and courage... you feel whole... connected...

You thank the cave for this experience before turning and walking towards the mouth of the cave... feeling a sense of wonder and awe at what you will see... as you reach the entrance to the cave you are amazed to see a night sky... and as you sit at the edge and look out you realise you can see nothing but that night sky and you realise you are at the centre of the universe itself... you see bright stars all around you... some near and some far away... some at the beginnings of their life cycle and some near the end... you see distant galaxies and the deep, dark depths of black holes... the sudden bright flash of comets... and planets with many moons... you sit for a moment... taking it all in... and as you do so you feel how everything is interconnected... and as you have that thought you see wispy strands of light between the stars and the planets and the moons... all the matter that you see... and you see that a strand of this reaches towards you yourself... connecting between your forehead... at your heart... and your womb space... you become aware of the rise and fall of your chest and belly as you breathe... and notice that as you are breathing the strands of light that connect you to everything shimmer with your breath... as if you are breathing the universe... or the universe breathing you... and for a few moments you continue to breathe this way... feeling safe... connected... and free...

And you can bring yourself back to your own breath, ready to return to your waking life, knowing that you can bring these new feelings and new consciousness with you… and when you return you will return refreshed and alert.

Take a few more moments to enjoy your special place before you begin to wake up… feeling calm and refreshed… and you will begin to wake up as I count from one to five… fully refreshed… calm and alert… one… beginning to come up… .two… becoming aware of the room around you… three… eyelids beginning to flicker… four… nearly there now… and five… OPEN YOUR EYES AND LOOK AROUND YOU, ALERT AND REFRESHED.

Spirituality of Birth

We looked at birth as a transformative process in the very first chapter, and the book comes full circle now to reiterate that this is not just a physical or psychological process but a spiritual one too. Many women have reported birth as being the catalyst for profound spiritual awakening.

This underlying spirituality of the birth process is recognised and felt strongly by many of those who work in the birth world, adding a whole extra dimension to what can only be described as a calling. I asked Nicola Goodall, a doula of some twenty-plus years in the UK, who trained with Michel Odent and is the founder of Red Tent Doulas, for her personal take on this topic, and she responded with this stunningly beautiful piece:

Birthkeepers
It is often assumed women are drawn to support birth because they 'like babies'. Certainly every other midwifery application is a young woman who wants that hit of chubby freshness in her life, but all the rest come to the work to support women and almost all of those feel some kind of calling: Divine if you like. The amount of applications I read through at Red Tent Doulas that contain that thread! Opportunities passed and reappearing. Synchronicities all over the place. I have come to a definite conclusion that there is some magic at play.

We walk alongside women as they travel this path to the next stage. From maiden to mother, from mother of sons to daughters, from mother to one partner's child to another, and often sadly from a society that says they should be judged for being gay parents, from a system that does not wholly support choice, experiencing what it is for a trauma survivor to give birth, through IVF, bodyshaming; whatever the circumstances we support all of their choices with no attachments and through this work we ourselves grow. We grow in our capacity to love and in our hope for the world. If we can bring in a new generation of babies that are born gently to women who can blossom and crack open and stand up and proudly move forward in life we can survive anything.

I see that women know to create life and to be a reflection of the Creator on earth and this is divine in its nature. Regardless of a belief in a higher being or not, to bring forth life is absolutely incredible! Women know they should be honoured and recognised during this holy time yet instead they are often met with an overstretched, poorly trained, burnt out system and a culture that frames the whole thing as a secular nightmare. We are the bridge. The birthkeepers are the faith bearers, the water bringers, the guardians of the sanctity, the ancient voice of wonder at the majesty of the mother. We are essential. This thread must never disappear. Without empowered healthy women, fathers and peaceful babies we are nothing as a species.

I prepare women to support other women as birthkeepers because I want reproductive justice. I want ALL women to feel empowered and not violated. I want to raise an army of women internationally that can each in turn raise their own army to smother this misogynistic, planet destroying energy we all have to suffer right now. To usher in the age of the Divine feminine where we can all play in the garden again. To survive in peace.

Nicola is a Muslim. Every email she sends ends with this most beautiful quote from the Qur'an: 'Paradise lies at the feet of the mothers.' Whatever your spiritual leanings, religion or even if you are a committed atheist, there is something about the primal power of the birthing woman that touches us all at the soul level, and this thread can be seen and reclaimed in all traditions and for all women. The 'Divine Feminine' that Nicola mentions is also known as the 'feminine face of God' whether experienced as the Jewish Shekinah, the Feminine attributes of Allah, the Holy Spirit, the Madonna, the Hindu Devi, the Buddhist Prajnaparamita, the Wiccan Triple Mother or simply a feeling that your innate creative power is both holy and connected to a force larger than you. The following guided journey is designed to help you begin to explore this for yourself.

Exercise – Goddess of Birth Visualisation

Just get yourself comfortable now... and now let your eyes find something on that wall... some spot or corner or a small object... and let your eyes rest on that point while you listen to the sound of my voice... hold your eyes open... and just look at that spot or that point... for a few moments... keep focusing on that spot... and your eyelids become heavy... heavier and heavier... blinking more and more... you can feel those eyelids becoming so heavy... but you just keep them open now... they may begin to water... that's okay... just keep them open... keep focusing... heavier and heavier... even though you want to close them you can keep them open for a few moments longer... and now close your eyes down... and as you close your eyes down you feel a wave of relaxation sweep through your entire body...

Now just focus on your breathing... breathing deeply... as you become so very deeply relaxed... breathing in... and breathing out... feeling your lungs and stomach expand as you breathe in... and your body relax so very deeply as you breathe out... relaxing more and more...

And now become aware of the quality of that relaxation...

and imagine that relaxation spreading through the whole of your body... sweeping down from the top of your head to the tips of your toes... like a wave of relaxation... letting go... let go and relax every muscle in your body... that's right... really feel that relaxation from the crown of your head to the tips of your toes... feel how very good it feels to be this deeply relaxed...

And as deep as you are now... you can go ten times deeper. In a moment I am going to ask you to open your eyes... and then when you close them again you will go ten times deeper... so very deeply relaxed... relaxed in body and mind...

When you are ready I want you to imagine... in as much detail as is right for you now... a stone staircase that takes you down to a special place... a safe place that is just for you... it feels inviting to you and you go down... a step at a time... as I count from ten to one... and as I do so you can imagine yourself going down... a step at a time... going deeper and deeper... ten... nine... eight... see yourself going down... seven... six... hear your footsteps on the stairs, feel the stairs beneath your feet, and imagine yourself going deeper still... five... four... three... two... one... you step down and you can find yourself in a cave... it is warm... and the stone walls all around you glow a soft, welcoming red... you get the impression that you are both inside your own womb and deep inside the centre of the Earth at the same time... and you just stop for a moment to enjoy this place... feeling safe and supported... nurtured and loved... and you become aware of a pulse beneath your feet... like a heartbeat... which seems to rise up through your body... through your veins... merging with the beating of your heart... just listen to this sound... the pulse of life... feeling yourself merge with the creative power of the Earth and even the universe itself... you feel a warm glow in your chest and it gives you strength, calm and courage... you feel whole... connected...

You stay here for a few moments before becoming aware of a presence all around you... a presence that feels loving and nurturing yet also primal and powerful, and somehow connected to the beat of your heart and the blood in your veins... feeling awed at this presence you sit down... waiting... you are not sure what you are waiting for, but you know She is coming...

You see a woman approaching you from the darkest shadows at the mouth of the cave... she walks with a purposeful and powerful gait... and the very air seems infused with reverence... as she comes towards you, you see her face... and you know her Name and you know she has wisdom for you that only She can impart... and for a few moments you will not hear the sound of my voice... but instead you find yourself talking to this Goddess, this woman who holds the secrets of the power of birth... and you take in all she has to tell you... and share with her all your fears, hopes and dreams...

(Pause here for a few minutes.)

When you are done, you thank her for all she has told you and you know that you will carry her wisdom in your heart and that you can call out to her at any time... and as she walks away back into the shadows you take a few moments to assimilate all you have heard and seen...

And you can bring yourself back to your breath now, ready to return to your waking life, knowing that you can bring these new feelings and new responses with you... and when you return you will return refreshed and alert.

Take a few more moments to enjoy your special place before you begin to wake up... feeling calm and refreshed... and you will begin to wake up as I count from one to five... fully refreshed... calm and alert... one... beginning to come up... two... becoming aware of the room around you... three... eyelids beginning to flicker... four... nearly there now... and five... OPEN YOUR EYES AND LOOK AROUND YOU, ALERT AND REFRESHED.

Resources/References

Childbirth and the Evolution of Homo Sapiens – Michel Odent (Pinter & Martin, 2013)

http://www.beginbeforebirth.org/the-science/epigenetics

The Biology of Belief – Bruce Lipton
http://birthingthefuture.org/
http://www.birthrights.org.uk/resources/videos/
http://whiteribbonalliance.org/
http://www.oneworldbirth.net/project/freedom-for-birth/
http://www.alternativesmagazine.com/38/spencer.html
https://www.youtube.com/watch?v=9uNHnbGkh4s – Nicola
Goodall's TEDx talk, 'Reframing Birth'
http://www.spiritualbirth.net/

Epilogue – Every Birth Matters; Woman-Centred Birth Around the World

The freedom of a country can be measured by its freedom of birth.
Agnes Gereb

We've spoken about how birth can change the future. What about right here, right now? Around the world many brave individuals and organisations are fighting for women's birth rights and compassionate care. It would be impossible to list all of these, so in this chapter I have given a snapshot of some of the most prominent or those that have touched my life in various ways, and provided resources to think about what you can do to support the global birth movement or even your own community, should you feel inspired to do so. Personally, I found it very empowering as a pregnant and new mother to know that I was part of something bigger than myself, a collective that at the same time honours each individual and their birthing experience. We started this book by looking at why birth matters; I end it having shown, I hope, that every birth matters.

UK – The Positive Birth Movement

The Positive Birth Movement, set up by Milli Hill, is a grassroots movement that aims to spread positive messages about birth and end the unnecessary culture of fear around childbirth, via groups of free antenatal classes focusing on positive birth, all linked up via social media. There are at the time of writing 250 PBM groups in the UK and 200 across the rest of the world, in 36 different countries.

The groups are based around discussion themes such as 'hopes and fears' or 'writing your birth plan' and although they are hosted by a facilitator, the aim is for women to learn from each other and support each other, not sitting and listening to an antenatal teacher. Facilitators may be birth professionals or simply a mother passionate about positive birth. The groups aim to complement, not replace, traditional antenatal teaching and help pregnant women absorb positive messages about birth and provide a warm and welcoming space. The movement's manifesto claims that a positive birth means:

- Choices are informed by reality not fear
- Women are listened to and treated with respect and dignity
- Mothers are empowered and enriched
- Memories are warm and proud

The movement is also aware that many women may have already experienced a less than positive birth, and encourage them to have their voices be heard at their sister project, All That Matters.

Get Involved
- Visit your local Positive Birth Group: http://www. positivebirthmovement.org/find-a-positive-birth-group. html
- If there isn't one, consider starting one! http:// www.positivebirthmovement.org/set-up-a-positive-birthgroup.html
- If you have had previous difficult birth experiences, get your voice heard at http://www.positivebirthmovement. org/all-that-matters-project.html

USA – Ina May Gaskin and The Farm

Ina May Gaskin has been described as 'the mother of authentic midwifery'. One of the foremost birth experts in the West, Ina May has devoted her life to the promotion of a return to natural, woman-centred birth processes and is the author of various bestselling books on birth, breastfeeding and midwifery, including the classic

Spiritual Midwifery, a must-read for anyone intending to get involved with birthwork. She was awarded the 'Right Livelihood' Award (also known as the 'Alternative Nobel Prize') in 2011.

In 1971, Ina May founded The Farm Midwifery Center, part of The Farm Community, an ecovillage committed to living in harmony with the Earth. As of 2011 the Midwifery Center had handled more than 3,000 births (1,200 by Ina May herself) with incredibly good outcomes and the lowest rates of interventions, morbidity and mortality across America, in spite of the fact many of those deliveries were multiples and/or breech. Women all over the US who had little other interest in the communal way of living The Farm promotes went there and still go there to deliver their babies, reassured by their remarkable statistics and the alternative to highly medicalised birth procedures that dominate in the US.

Ina May has been awarded a Doctorate by Thames Valley UIna May has been awarded a Doctorate by Thames Valley University in London and been made a Fellow of Yale University, in recognition of her outstanding contribution to midwifery practice. She is the only midwife to have an obstetric practice named after her – the Gaskin Maneuver, a low intervention but extremely effective method for dealing with shoulder dystocia (where the shoulder becomes stuck after the baby's head is delivered). Ina May has influenced much of modern birth work and continues to do so, although she is at the time of writing seventy-seven years old!

Find out more
- *https://www.youtube.com/watch?v=S9LO1Vb54yk*
- *If you live anywhere near Tennessee, you might want to consider having your baby at The Farm! http://thefarmmidwives.org/ delivering-your-baby/*

The Netherlands – Encouraging Home Birth

Although no country can claim a Utopia when it comes to birthing practices, the Dutch model is highly lauded in the West for its high rate of home births – nearly a third of all births – and its attitude toward woman-centred birth. Where there are no complications present childbirth is seen, rightly, as a natural physiological event and not a medical emergency. As a result intervention rates, including epidural, are low. Natural pain relief is expected and encouraged, with midwives actively recommending prenatal yoga and hypnobirthing. The emphasis is on keeping risk and intervention down and giving the mother freedom, choice and safe places to birth. Though not without its challenges, the Dutch maternity model is one the rest of the Western world would do well to emulate.

India – MATRIKA

MATRIKA stands for Motherhood and Traditional Resources, Information, Knowledge and Action. It was set up by Janet Chawla, who found when teaching natural childbirth classes in Delhi that women were not having the births they had prepared for due to unnecessary obstetric intervention. They also felt their needs went largely ignored by medical staff. Using funding from UNICEF among others, MATRIKA was set up as an NGO to reclaim indigenous midwifery practices and bring them back to the birthing room, by pioneering a new way of training birth attendants that consulted traditional practitioners, utilised active listening and positive reinforcement and focused on the question: 'What do women need?'

Find out more at http://matrika-india.org/Matrika.php.

Hungary – Agnes Gereb and the Home Birth Movement

Until recently (and it is still incredibly difficult) a midwife in Hungary could not obtain a legal licence to attend a home birth.

Therefore, although the healthcare system in Hungary professed to offer a free choice to women in where to give birth, by making access to midwives unobtainable they left women with the choice of a freebirth (unattended by a trained birth professional) or a highly medicalised hospital birth. The Home Birth Movement was set up and many midwives such as Agnes Gereb continued to attend home births anyway. Despite Agnes also being a trained obstetrician and gynaecologist and a recognised expert in home birth having safely delivered over 3,500 babies at home, the authorities criminalised her work and have placed her both in jail and under house arrest. In spite of numerous appeals and global support, after the death of a newborn following complication Agnes still faces prosecution for reckless endangerment. Her story is the focus of the film *Freedom for Birth*. Although maternity services are slowly changing in Hungary, progress is slow, and Agnes Gereb has become a figurehead for home birth campaigners across the world.

Get Involved
- *Watch and share* Freedom for Birth: *www.oneworldbirth.net/ project/freedom-for-birth/*
- *Keep up to date on Agnes' case and offer your support: http:// legalfunddragnesgereb.net/landing-page/court-cases/*

Mexico – Rural Midwifery

Rates of home births are high in Mexico, particularly in rural areas, and so many traditional birth practices are very much alive – a factor that is beginning to influence hospital care, where rates of episiotomy and Caesarean remain high. More midwife-led birthing centres such as Casa Aramara are being built and there is a move towards training student midwives in the traditional practices of lay rural midwives (largely due to concern that lay midwifery may die out as many of these traditional midwives are advanced in age).

A word on Rebozos

A traditional Mesoamerican practice that is gaining in popularity the world over is that of using the Rebozo as a birth aid. A Rebozo is a traditionally woven Mexican shawl, which you are wrapped in at birth, use during your life – including during labour and as a baby sling – and are wrapped in again at death. They have also become a revolutionary symbol and are often associated in the West with the figure of artists and revolutionary Frida Kahlo. Rebozos are used for various movements that help a labouring woman – such as the 'Double Hip Squeeze' and 'Shaking the Apples' where the hips are jiggled with the scarf. Although these techniques are undoubtedly helpful in labour, many Mexican people are understandably angry at the way the West has appropriated the Rebozo. You can now go to classes led by women who have probably never been to Mexico or Mesoamerica in their life teaching you Rebozo as a birth aid, using a 'Rebozo' made cheaply in China! Any shawl or scarf can be used for these practices; after all active movement in labour originated in all cultures, but the word 'Rebozo' should only be used if the garment has been properly sourced and the techniques are being taught by an indigenous practitioner, not by a facilitator on a weekend course who has no idea of the cultural significance of the garment but is using the term to charge a hefty price. Find out more about these issues at https://www.youtube.com/watch?v=-FLpizSdX-M.

Philippines – Ibu Robin Lim

Robin Lim is a world-renowned midwife, a passionate advocate of woman-centred birth and was awarded the BirthKeeper of the Year Award in 2012 from the Association of Prenatal and Perinatal Psychological Health. She describes herself as following in the footsteps of her Filipino grandmother who was a traditional birth attendant. Robin is celebrated for her work with marginalised people and is involved in various charitable foundations. She is the founder of Yayasan Bumi Sehat (Healthy Mother Earth Foundation) in Indonesia and Wanita dan Harapan (Women and Hope) in the Philippines. An award-winning documentary, *Guerrilla Midwife*, has been made about Ibu Robin and her work, and I would recommend this to all mothers and women interested in the birth process. Find out more, as well as ways to get involved, at http://www. bumisehatfoundation.org/other-ways-to-give/.

Every Mother Counts

Every Mother Counts is an organisation which aims to make birth safer for women and reduce rates of mortality, both in the developing world where a woman dies in childbirth every 2 minutes, and in the US which has one of the worst maternity rates in the West. EMC provides training for midwives in Syria, Guatemala, Bangladesh, Haiti and Tanzania, trains activists and lawyers in India to fight maternal health violations and runs Commonsense Childbirth in Florida, providing prenatal care and childbirth education for high-risk and low-income mothers in the area.

They have raised money to provide solar power for maternity clinics in Malawi and Nepal, donated medical supplies to clinics in the Democratic Republic of Congo and set up Ancient Song Doula Services in New York, providing doula services and training to low-income women of colour in the area.

What you can do:
- *Buy products from companies that support Every Mother Counts: https://www.everymothercounts.org/pages/shop*
- *Get fit and raise money at the same time: https://www. everymothercounts.org/pages/run*
- *Sign petitions calling for improved maternal health care: https:// www.change.org/p/cover-midwife-and-doula-services-for-mothers-in-the-united-states-givingbirthinamerica*

Appendix A – Positive Birth Stories

Shaney Leigh's Water Birth

Whilst pregnant and looking into my options I always knew I wanted a water birth. I followed the practices of hypnobirthing and tried to stay active and positive during my pregnancy. When I went into labour I was 6 days 'overdue'. My contractions started around seven in the evening and by midnight they were three minutes apart. I went to the hospital but was sent home as I was dilated to two centimetres and therefore not in active labour. I went home and ran myself a bath. I concentrated on my breathing and remaining calm. The bath brought on my contractions very swiftly and I started to have the sensation to push, as well as the appearance of the plug. At this point my contractions were around a minute and a half apart and we dashed back off to the hospital. It was now about three-thirty in the morning. It was a bit of a mad dash as I was pushing and had to be carried in, but I got set up in the birthing suite and given some gas and air and was easily able to relax myself and control the sensations to push. I felt in control again and looked forward to getting in the pool. I was five centimetres dilated and in active labour so good to stay! While they ran the pool for me I was on all fours on the bean bag concentrating on my breathing and using gas and air. I got in the pool at four am and it was such a relief to be able to move around comfortably and feel weightless in between contractions. It was only a short half an hour later that I was fully dilated and ready to push. Throughout this time I felt relaxed and in control. My partner was fantastic. He didn't 'do' much but that was exactly what I wanted! He didn't get in the way but let me get on with it and stay in my zone while just letting me know he was there for me. After a few pushes my daughter was born and I was the one that lifted her out of the water into my arms. I was shocked at how quick it had all been and felt so empowered with what I had just achieved! We had immediate skin on skin and delayed cord clamping. After a while my partner cut the cord, checked baby over and handed her to Daddy. I was helped out of the pool and delivered the placenta naturally.

Jan's Pain-free Birth

Our due date was Wednesday 31st August but at 11.45pm on Monday 29th August my waters broke at home. I was laying in bed feeling like I was about to wet myself but made it to the loo – it was a surreal feeling knowing what my body was starting to do! As it was late at night I tried going to bed but an hour later I had a big contraction, my first one. I'd been up and down to the loo with an upset tummy and I had started to bleed; I rang the hospital and they said to come in. I had no more contractions at home. I had a few in the car and I remember telling my husband to shut up as he was trying to take my mind off my discomfort! We went into the midwife-led birthing suite where I was still contracting but not too often, and we were sent to go for a walk. I decided I wanted some fresh air – we got outside OK and my contractions were more and more frequent – I felt really warm and hubby was getting cold! After a while I thought I had better attempt the long walk back to the ward – all I can say is I'm glad there are handrails all along the corridors – I think I had to stop 3–4 times and Paul was amazing by massaging my back and making me sway (the only thing we learnt in antenatal classes that I actually used!). When we got back in our room I couldn't settle at all, I tried the birthing ball, chair and beanbag and all were uncomfy. At 4.26am a doctor came to examine me and said I was fully dilated! I was taken onto the delivery ward and into room 4 where at 4.34am I started pushing. All of our hospital bags were still in the car!

Luckily I had a bottle of water and lip balm which got me through it but I would have loved an eye mask and a fan!

The midwife said I was pushing really well and I remember remarking that I felt no pain at all even though I had no pain relief. She said I was just so focused on getting my baby girl out.

I tried pushing whilst on my knees but I didn't find it comfortable so after two contractions and pushes I went back onto my back, completely against the National Childbirth Trust teachings! My baby came out on the next push so she was born exactly at 7am on Tuesday 30th August!

I cut her cord as Paul was too squeamish! But he examined the placenta with the midwife and was fascinated by his science lesson!

I loved my positive birthing experience, I know I'm very lucky to have breezed through it all!

Corrinne's VBA2C (Vaginal Birth after two Caesareans)

I had both my daughters prematurely so when I woke up during my third pregnancy at 30+2 weeks having contractions 5 minutes apart I was worried but not surprised. I phoned the independent midwife I had booked and went into hospital. The monitor showed I was contracting steadily but I wasn't dilating as I have cervical stenosis. I was given steroids – but no pain relief! – and taken up to labour ward. I spent the day contracting on and off and wasn't given pain relief as I couldn't be classed as in labour because I wasn't dilating due to the stenosis! I couldn't help thinking, 'Well, doh!' By 10pm I was contracting every 2 minutes and the doctor wanted me to have a Caesarean. I was on the verge of it, then I was given gas and air which helped me relax and everything changed. I started singing David Bowie! The baby was doing fine and then I knew – I was going to get the VBAC I had wanted! At 2am my cervix was completely effaced but because of the stenosis I hadn't dilated. My midwife reached in and pressed on my cervix during a contraction and it popped open to 5 cms! By 8.30am I was 10 cm and I didn't feel scared – I felt ready. I pushed my daughter out in 26 minutes and was able to hold her before she was taken to the Special Care Unit as she was so premature. It was such an empowering experience; I felt strong and healed by having the natural delivery I craved. We brought our daughter home a few weeks later and I couldn't have been prouder! The independent midwife was amazing, gas and air is great and I felt as though we were protected and supported by the Universe throughout.

Kathy's Home Birth

There was never any question in my mind that I wanted a home birth. My mother had me and my sisters at home and I was at my sister's home birth with my niece. My aunt is a midwife and hypnobirthing teacher. I was very lucky in that unlike all of my friends my family's stories around birth were all positive and encouraging. What I wasn't prepared for was how obstructive the doctors and midwives would be; citing everything from being short staffed to me 'being naïve' about the risks! I couldn't afford an independent midwife, so I had to put my foot down and insist on a home birth, and just prayed that the midwife on call would be on board with what I wanted. As it happened she was fantastic; but only just arrived on time! I woke up on the morning of my 'due date' with crampy niggles and lower back ache and the baby feeling very low and heavy. This lasted all day, but although I thought it might mean I would go into labour soon I had no idea that it was already happening! I suddenly started getting intense contractions and my waters broke at 7pm and I called the maternity unit for the midwife. She was there within half an hour, but I was crowning as she walked in the door! I had spent the time sitting on the birthing ball with my partner behind me, rocking and chanting my favourite yoga mantra. I wouldn't describe the contractions as painful, but they were so intense they blocked all else out but my immediate physical experience; it felt very 'primal'. The midwife looked panicked when she came in but soon she was holding my hand and encouraging me as I delivered my son's head and body in just a few pushes. My partner burst into tears as he was laid on my chest and held us both as the midwife wiped our son down and he began to suckle, squinting up at me with one eye open.

Mary's Gentle Caesarean

I was scheduled for surgery at 38 weeks after a 35-week scan showed placenta praevia (where the placenta lies across the cervix). Although I was disappointed as I had wanted another natural delivery I had known since the 20-week scan this was a possibility and so had been researching ways to make a Caesarean more 'natural'. I hired a doula to be with us postnatally. My consultant was lovely and very receptive to my wishes. The only thing I was frightened of was having the spinal block administered, so I went to a hypnotherapist for a few sessions and learned self-hypnosis techniques to keep me calm, and also had hypnosis to promote my body's natural healing powers to aid my recovery from the surgery. I woke up on the morning nervous but excited. The calming techniques I had learned worked wonders for the spinal block and I felt relaxed and warm during the procedure – feeling nothing but some tugging sensations. I had asked to be told when our son was about to emerge so I could imagine and visualise pushing and giving birth, and I had the drapes lowered as he was lifted out. Seeing his head emerge from my belly was amazing. He was placed on me immediately and literally crawled up my breasts to root straight for the nipple! We were wrapped up in a warm shawl while I was stitched up, and didn't cut the cord until it had stopped pulsating. It was a beautiful experience. My physical recovery was swift and the doula was amazing – she cooked for us, gave me shoulder rubs when they were aching from breastfeeding and kept my husband calm! Having an extra pair of hands really helped me relax, recover and enjoy those precious first weeks.

Chantel's Natural Twin Birth

I felt really pressured by my consultant to have an elective Caesarean at 37 weeks, but I knew I wanted a natural birth and it was really important to me and my husband. My babies were healthy and in good position so I saw no reason why I couldn't deliver them myself. When I told the consultant this I was told they couldn't guarantee having a midwife on the ward that was experienced in natural twin birth! That seemed to me an inadequate reason to have an elective Caesarean. I booked a doula and an independent midwife and pushed for a natural delivery. My consultant wasn't happy, but it was my birth, not his! I went into labour at 38 and a half weeks and was at home for two days, having frequent but mild contractions and lots of lovely massages from my husband! My doula was great and I felt really loved and supported. By the end of the second day I wasn't progressing and my waters hadn't broken so I decided to transfer to the hospital. The babies must have known, because on the way there my waters went and contractions ramped up. Within two hours of arriving I gave birth to two beautiful girls, leaning over a birthing ball with gas and air. It was painful and intense but very quick and I felt so empowered and glad I had trusted my instincts. I had my babies laying on my chest while I delivered the placenta and I remember thinking how amazing birth was; and that I wanted to do it all again!

Appendix B – Suggestions for a Mother Blessing Ritual

Birth is a woman's spiritual vision quest. When this idea is ritualised beforehand, the deeper meanings of childbirth can more readily be accessed.
Jeanine Parvati-Baker

You can have a doula or ritual leader hold a blessing party or simply get a like-minded friend on board. Like the more commercialised concept of a 'baby shower' a mother blessing is a gathering of the pregnant woman and her – predominantly female – friends, to celebrate and honour the pregnancy and bless the coming birth. A mother blessing is more focused on just that: the honouring and blessing, rather than gifts or swapping advice and often horrific birth stories! It can be adapted to all religions and cultures and individual tastes, so what follows is a basic template that will give you some ideas for your own or a friend's ceremony.

Set-up
You might want to prepare a ritual space by setting up an altar, decorating the room with lights, cushions, fabrics etc. An ideal layout would be everyone sits in a circle with an altar or centrepiece in the middle – or alternatively put the pregnant woman in the centre! Items you might like on the altar include fresh fruit, flowers, depictions of pregnancy, photos and gifts for the soon-to-be mother. Ask everyone to bring healthy home-cooked food to share and perhaps also a creative offering or any gift they wish to give.

Opening
You may like to welcome the woman in with a special song or dance, or even by creating a tunnel with your hands for her

to pass through. Once everyone is comfy, officially open the ceremony by declaring why you are there. Go round the circle and ask each woman to introduce themselves and say a few loving words to the mother, perhaps sharing a memory of their friendship or the thing they most admire about her.

Reading
A poetry or passage can be read honouring and celebrating birth. This may be something you have sourced or written yourself. Alternatively each woman brings something short and takes it in turns to read out. As well as or instead of a reading you might like to do a dance or pregnancy appropriate yoga sequence.

Healing
The woman speaks of her hopes and fears and wishes for the coming birth, and the circle holds space, listening with compassion. When she has finished, each woman says to her, 'I hear you, I see you, you are loved.'

Meditation
The host leads a guided meditation centred around birth and creation and life. You can use the 'birth journey' visualisation in Chapter One for this, or any of the guided visualisations you feel are appropriate.

Creating
You may like to add a creative component where everyone crafts a small talisman or piece of birth art or even colouring.

Celebration
Get out the food! Play music, talk, laugh, dance.

Blessing and Closing
Each woman voices her blessing for the mother and baby, and

gives her gift if she has one, perhaps touching the mother's stomach as she voices her blessing. Or the woman can lie in the middle and everyone places a hand on her stomach, voicing their blessing in turn. When this is done, declare the closing with a short general blessing or chant and hug!

Examples of Chants and Poems

Opening
'You're welcome, you're welcome
   We see you in the circle and we welcome you' (repeat as desired).

Reading
'Growing
Unfolding
Becoming
Beholding
New life bursts forth
Nourished
Blessed
Loved
Welcomed
Change blossoms within you
This is the birth season.
The sap is rising
The tide is rising
Womanpower rising
This is the birth season
This is the ending
This is the beginning
This is the journey
This is the birth season.'

Closing Blessing (Old Irish)
'Deep Peace of the running wave to you
Deep Peace of the flowing air to you
Deep Peace of the quiet earth to you
Deep Peace of the shining stars to you.'

Acknowledgments

The first birth I ever attended was a stillbirth. I couldn't have known it at the time, but the witnessing of both a miracle and a tragedy in the same moment was an early factor that led to my becoming a birthkeeper. To that woman and her child, my thoughts and prayers eternally.

To my own babies, the living and the lost, you are my greatest loves and my greatest teachers.

My mother, grandmother, great-grandmother and beyond. May I continue to learn from both your wisdom and your mistakes.

To all the wonderful women the world over who never stop believing. You are the ones we have been waiting for.

BOOKS

O-BOOKS

SPIRITUALITY

O is a symbol of the world, of oneness and unity; this eye represents knowledge and insight. We publish titles on general spirituality and living a spiritual life. We aim to inform and help you on your own journey in this life.

If you have enjoyed this book, why not tell other readers by posting a review on your preferred book site? Recent bestsellers from O-Books are:

Heart of Tantric Sex
Diana Richardson
Revealing Eastern secrets of deep love and intimacy to Western couples.
Paperback: 978-1-90381-637-0 ebook: 978-1-84694-637-0

Crystal Prescriptions
The A-Z guide to over 1,200 symptoms and their healing crystals
Judy Hall
The first in the popular series of six books, this handy little guide is packed as tight as a pill-bottle with crystal remedies for ailments.
Paperback: 978-1-90504-740-6 ebook: 978-1-84694-629-5

Take Me To Truth
Undoing the Ego
Nouk Sanchez, Tomas Vieira
The best-selling step-by-step book on shedding the Ego, using the
teachings of A Course In Miracles.
Paperback: 978-1-84694-050-7 ebook: 978-1-84694-654-7

The 7 Myths about Love...Actually!
The journey from your HEAD to the HEART of your SOUL
Mike George
Smashes all the myths about LOVE.
Paperback: 978-1-84694-288-4 ebook: 978-1-84694-682-0

The Holy Spirit's Interpretation of the New Testament
A course in Understanding and Acceptance
Regina Dawn Akers
Following on from the strength of *A Course In Miracles*, NTI
teaches us how to experience the love and oneness of God.
Paperback: 978-1-84694-085-9 ebook: 978-1-78099-083-5

The Message of A Course In Miracles
A translation of the text in plain language
Elizabeth A. Cronkhite
A translation of *A Course in Miracles* into plain, everyday
language for anyone seeking inner peace. The companion
volume, *Practicing A Course In Miracles*, offers practical lessons
and mentoring.
Paperback: 978-1-84694-319-5 ebook: 978-1-84694-642-4

Thinker's Guide to God
Peter Vardy
An introduction to key issues in the philosophy of religion.
Paperback: 978-1-90381-622-6

Your Simple Path
Find happiness in every step
Ian Tucker
A guide to helping us reconnect with what is really important in our lives.
Paperback: 978-1-78279-349-6 ebook: 978-1-78279-348-9

365 Days of Wisdom
Daily Messages To Inspire You Through The Year
Dadi Janki
Daily messages which cool the mind, warm the heart and guide you along your journey.
Paperback: 978-1-84694-863-3 ebook: 978-1-84694-864-0

Body of Wisdom
Women's Spiritual Power and How it Serves
Hilary Hart
Bringing together the dreams and experiences of women across the world with today's most visionary spiritual teachers.
Paperback: 978-1-78099-696-7 ebook: 978-1-78099-695-0

Dying to Be Free
From Enforced Secrecy to Near Death to True Transformation
Hannah Robinson
After an unexpected accident and near-death experience, Hannah Robinson found herself radically transforming her life, while a remarkable new insight altered her relationship with her father, a practising Catholic priest.
Paperback: 978-1-78535-254-6 ebook: 978-1-78535-255-3

The Ecology of the Soul

A Manual of Peace, Power and Personal Growth for Real People
in the Real World
Aidan Walker
Balance your own inner Ecology of the Soul to regain your
natural state of peace, power and wellbeing.
Paperback: 978-1-78279-850-7 ebook: 978-1-78279-849-1

Not I, Not other than I

The Life and Teachings of Russel Williams
Steve Taylor, Russel Williams
The miraculous life and inspiring teachings of one of the World's
greatest living Sages.
Paperback: 978-1-78279-729-6 ebook: 978-1-78279-728-9

On the Other Side of Love

A Woman's Unconventional Journey Towards Wisdom
Muriel Maufroy
When life has lost all meaning, what do you do?
Paperback: 978-1-78535-281-2 ebook: 978-1-78535-282-9

Practicing A Course In Miracles

A Translation of the Workbook in Plain Language and With
Mentoring Notes
Elizabeth A. Cronkhite
The practical second and third volumes of The Plain-Language A
Course In Miracles.
Paperback: 978-1-84694-403-1 ebook: 978-1-78099-072-9

Quantum Bliss

The Quantum Mechanics of Happiness, Abundance, and Health

George S. Mentz

Quantum Bliss is the breakthrough summary of success and spirituality secrets that customers have been waiting for.

Paperback: 978-1-78535-203-4 ebook: 978-1-78535-204-1

The Upside Down Mountain

Mags MacKean

A must-read for anyone weary of chasing success and happiness – one woman's inspirational journey swapping the uphill slog for the downhill slope.

Paperback: 978-1-78535-171-6 ebook: 978-1-78535-172-3

Your Personal Tuning Fork

The Endocrine System

Deborah Bates

Discover your body's health secret, the endocrine system, and 'twang' your way to sustainable health!

Paperback: 978-1-84694-503-8 ebook: 978-1-78099-697-4

Readers of ebooks can buy or view any of these bestsellers by clicking on the live link in the title. Most titles are published in paperback and as an ebook. Paperbacks are available in traditional bookshops. Both print and ebook formats are available online.

Find more titles and sign up to our readers' newsletter at http://www.johnhuntpublishing.com/mind-body-spirit

Follow us on Facebook at https://www.facebook.com/OBooks/ and Twitter at https://twitter.com/obooks